Samples and Populations

Data and Statistics

Glenda Lappan
James T. Fey
William M. Fitzgerald
Susan N. Friel
Elizabeth Difanis Phillips

Boston, Massachusetts · Glenview, Illinois · Shoreview, Minnesota · Upper Saddle River, New Jersey

Connected Mathematics™ was developed at Michigan State University with financial support from the Michigan State University Office of the Provost, Computing and Technology, and the College of Natural Science.

This material is based upon work supported by the National Science Foundation under Grant No. MDR 9150217 and Grant No. ESI 9986372. Opinions expressed are those of the authors and not necessarily those of the Foundation.

The Michigan State University authors and administration have agreed that all MSU royalties arising from this publication will be devoted to purposes supported by the MSU Mathematics Education Enrichment Fund.

Acknowledgments appear on page 95, which constitutes an extension of this copyright page.

13-digit ISBN 978-0-13-366157-6
10-digit ISBN 0-13-366157-1
7 8 9 10 V003 15 14 13 12

Authors of Connected Mathematics

(from left to right) Glenda Lappan, Betty Phillips, Susan Friel, Bill Fitzgerald, Jim Fey

Glenda Lappan is a University Distinguished Professor in the Department of Mathematics at Michigan State University. Her research and development interests are in the connected areas of students' learning of mathematics and mathematics teachers' professional growth and change related to the development and enactment of K–12 curriculum materials.

James T. Fey is a Professor of Curriculum and Instruction and Mathematics at the University of Maryland. His consistent professional interest has been development and research focused on curriculum materials that engage middle and high school students in problem-based collaborative investigations of mathematical ideas and their applications.

William M. Fitzgerald *(Deceased)* was a Professor in the Department of Mathematics at Michigan State University. His early research was on the use of concrete materials in supporting student learning and led to the development of teaching materials for laboratory environments. Later he helped develop a teaching model to support student experimentation with mathematics.

Susan N. Friel is a Professor of Mathematics Education in the School of Education at the University of North Carolina at Chapel Hill. Her research interests focus on statistics education for middle-grade students and, more broadly, on teachers' professional development and growth in teaching mathematics K–8.

Elizabeth Difanis Phillips is a Senior Academic Specialist in the Mathematics Department of Michigan State University. She is interested in teaching and learning mathematics for both teachers and students. These interests have led to curriculum and professional development projects at the middle school and high school levels, as well as projects related to the teaching and learning of algebra across the grades.

Field Test Sites for CMP2

During the development of the revised edition of *Connected Mathematics* (CMP2), more than 100 classroom teachers have field-tested materials at 49 school sites in 12 states and the District of Columbia. This classroom testing occurred over three academic years (2001 through 2004), allowing careful study of the effectiveness of each of the 24 units that comprise the program. A special thanks to the students and teachers at these pilot schools.

Arkansas
Magnolia Public Schools
Kittena Bell*, Judith Trowell*; *Central Elementary School:* Maxine Broom, Betty Eddy, Tiffany Fallin, Bonnie Flurry, Carolyn Monk, Elizabeth Tye; *Magnolia Junior High School:* Monique Bryan, Ginger Cook, David Graham, Shelby Lamkin

Colorado
Boulder Public Schools
Nevin Platt Middle School: Judith Koenig

St. Vrain Valley School District, Longmont
Westview Middle School: Colleen Beyer, Kitty Canupp, Ellie Decker*, Peggy McCarthy, Tanya deNobrega, Cindy Payne, Ericka Pilon, Andrew Roberts

District of Columbia
Capitol Hill Day School: Ann Lawrence

Georgia
University of Georgia, Athens
Brad Findell
Madison Public Schools
Morgan County Middle School: Renee Burgdorf, Lynn Harris, Nancy Kurtz, Carolyn Stewart

Maine
Falmouth Public Schools
Falmouth Middle School: Donna Erikson, Joyce Hebert, Paula Hodgkins, Rick Hogan, David Legere, Cynthia Martin, Barbara Stiles, Shawn Towle*

Michigan
Portland Public Schools
Portland Middle School: Mark Braun, Holly DeRosia, Kathy Dole*, Angie Foote, Teri Keusch, Tammi Wardwell

Traverse City Area Public Schools
Bertha Vos Elementary: Kristin Sak; *Central Grade School:* Michelle Clark; Jody Meyers; *Eastern Elementary:* Karrie Tufts; *Interlochen Elementary:* Mary McGee-Cullen; *Long Lake Elementary:* Julie Faulkner*, Charlie Maxbauer, Katherine Sleder; *Norris Elementary:* Hope Slanaker; *Oak Park Elementary:* Jessica Steed; *Traverse Heights Elementary:* Jennifer Wolfert; *Westwoods Elementary:* Nancy Conn; *Old Mission Peninsula School:* Deb Larimer; *Traverse City East Junior High:* Ivanka Berkshire, Ruthanne Kladder, Jan Palkowski, Jane Peterson, Mary Beth Schmitt; *Traverse City West Junior High:* Dan Fouch*, Ray Fouch

Sturgis Public Schools
Sturgis Middle School: Ellen Eisele

Minnesota
Burnsville School District 191
Hidden Valley Elementary: Stephanie Cin, Jane McDevitt

Hopkins School District 270
Alice Smith Elementary: Sandra Cowing, Kathleen Gustafson, Martha Mason, Scott Stillman; *Eisenhower Elementary:* Chad Bellig, Patrick Berger, Nancy Glades, Kye Johnson, Shane Wasserman, Victoria Wilson; *Gatewood Elementary:* Sarah Ham, Julie Kloos, Janine Pung, Larry Wade; *Glen Lake Elementary:* Jacqueline Cramer, Kathy Hering, Cecelia Morris, Robb Trenda; *Katherine Curren Elementary:* Diane Bancroft, Sue DeWit, John Wilson; *L. H. Tanglen Elementary:* Kevin Athmann, Lisa Becker, Mary LaBelle, Kathy Rezac, Roberta Severson; *Meadowbrook Elementary:* Jan Gauger, Hildy Shank, Jessica Zimmerman; *North Junior High:* Laurel Hahn, Kristin Lee, Jodi Markuson, Bruce Mestemacher, Laurel Miller, Bonnie Rinker, Jeannine Salzer, Sarah Shafer, Cam Stottler; *West Junior High:* Alicia Beebe, Kristie Earl, Nobu Fujii, Pam Georgetti, Susan Gilbert, Regina Nelson Johnson, Debra Lindstrom, Michele Luke*, Jon Sorenson

Minneapolis School District 1
Ann Sullivan K-8 School: Bronwyn Collins; Anne Bartel* (Curriculum and Instruction Office)

Wayzata School District 284
Central Middle School: Sarajane Myers, Dan Nielsen, Tanya Ravenholdt

White Bear Lake School District 624
Central Middle School: Amy Jorgenson, Michelle Reich, Brenda Sammon

New York
New York City Public Schools
IS 89: Yelena Aynbinder, Chi-Man Ng, Nina Rapaport, Joel Spengler, Phyllis Tam*, Brent Wyso; *Wagner Middle School:* Jason Appel, Intissar Fernandez, Yee Gee Get, Richard Goldstein, Irving Marcus, Sue Norton, Bernadita Owens, Jennifer Rehn*, Kevin Yuhas

---

* indicates a Field Test Site Coordinator

Ohio

Talawanda School District, Oxford
Talawanda Middle School: Teresa Abrams, Larry Brock, Heather Brosey, Julie Churchman, Monna Even, Karen Fitch, Bob George, Amanda Klee, Pat Meade, Sandy Montgomery, Barbara Sherman, Lauren Steidl

Miami University
Jeffrey Wanko*

Springfield Public Schools
Rockway School: Jim Mamer

Pennsylvania

Pittsburgh Public Schools
Kenneth Labuskes, Marianne O'Connor, Mary Lynn Raith*; *Arthur J. Rooney Middle School:* David Hairston, Stamatina Mousetis, Alfredo Zangaro; *Frick International Studies Academy:* Suzanne Berry, Janet Falkowski, Constance Finseth, Romika Hodge, Frank Machi; *Reizenstein Middle School:* Jeff Baldwin, James Brautigam, Lorena Burnett, Glen Cobbett, Michael Jordan, Margaret Lazur, Melissa Munnell, Holly Neely, Ingrid Reed, Dennis Reft

Texas

Austin Independent School District
Bedichek Middle School: Lisa Brown, Jennifer Glasscock, Vicki Massey

El Paso Independent School District
Cordova Middle School: Armando Aguirre, Anneliesa Durkes, Sylvia Guzman, Pat Holguin*, William Holguin, Nancy Nava, Laura Orozco, Michelle Peña, Roberta Rosen, Patsy Smith, Jeremy Wolf

Plano Independent School District
Patt Henry, James Wohlgehagen*; *Frankford Middle School:* Mandy Baker, Cheryl Butsch, Amy Dudley, Betsy Eshelman, Janet Greene, Cort Haynes, Kathy Letchworth, Kay Marshall, Kelly McCants, Amy Reck, Judy Scott, Syndy Snyder, Lisa Wang; *Wilson Middle School:* Darcie Bane, Amanda Bedenko, Whitney Evans, Tonelli Hatley, Sarah (Becky) Higgs, Kelly Johnston, Rebecca McElligott, Kay Neuse, Cheri Slocum, Kelli Straight

Washington

Evergreen School District
Shahala Middle School: Nicole Abrahamsen, Terry Coon*, Carey Doyle, Sheryl Drechsler, George Gemma, Gina Helland, Amy Hilario, Darla Lidyard, Sean McCarthy, Tilly Meyer, Willow Neuwelt, Todd Parsons, Brian Pederson, Stan Posey, Shawn Scott, Craig Sjoberg, Lynette Sundstrom, Charles Switzer, Luke Youngblood

Wisconsin

Beaver Dam Unified School District
Beaver Dam Middle School: Jim Braemer, Jeanne Frick, Jessica Greatens, Barbara Link, Dennis McCormick, Karen Michels, Nancy Nichols*, Nancy Palm, Shelly Stelsel, Susan Wiggins

---

* indicates a Field Test Site Coordinator

Reviews of CMP to Guide Development of CMP2

Before writing for CMP2 began or field tests were conducted, the first edition of *Connected Mathematics* was submitted to the mathematics faculties of school districts from many parts of the country and to 80 individual reviewers for extensive comments.

School District Survey Reviews of CMP

Arizona
Madison School District #38 (Phoenix)

Arkansas
Cabot School District, Little Rock School District, Magnolia School District

California
Los Angeles Unified School District

Colorado
St. Vrain Valley School District (Longmont)

Florida
Leon County Schools (Tallahassee)

Illinois
School District #21 (Wheeling)

Indiana
Joseph L. Block Junior High (East Chicago)

Kentucky
Fayette County Public Schools (Lexington)

Maine
Selection of Schools

Massachusetts
Selection of Schools

Michigan
Sparta Area Schools

Minnesota
Hopkins School District

Texas
Austin Independent School District, The El Paso Collaborative for Academic Excellence, Plano Independent School District

Wisconsin
Platteville Middle School

Individual Reviewers of CMP

Arkansas
Deborah Cramer; Robby Frizzell *(Taylor)*; Lowell Lynde *(University of Arkansas, Monticello)*; Leigh Manzer *(Norfork)*; Lynne Roberts *(Emerson High School, Emerson)*; Tony Timms *(Cabot Public Schools)*; Judith Trowell *(Arkansas Department of Higher Education)*

California
José Alcantar *(Gilroy)*; Eugenie Belcher *(Gilroy)*; Marian Pasternack *(Lowman M. S. T. Center, North Hollywood)*; Susana Pezoa *(San Jose)*; Todd Rabusin *(Hollister)*; Margaret Siegfried *(Ocala Middle School, San Jose)*; Polly Underwood *(Ocala Middle School, San Jose)*

Colorado
Janeane Golliher *(St. Vrain Valley School District, Longmont)*; Judith Koenig *(Nevin Platt Middle School, Boulder)*

Florida
Paige Loggins *(Swift Creek Middle School, Tallahassee)*

Illinois
Jan Robinson *(School District #21, Wheeling)*

Indiana
Frances Jackson *(Joseph L. Block Junior High, East Chicago)*

Kentucky
Natalee Feese *(Fayette County Public Schools, Lexington)*

Maine
Betsy Berry *(Maine Math & Science Alliance, Augusta)*

Maryland
Joseph Gagnon *(University of Maryland, College Park)*; Paula Maccini *(University of Maryland, College Park)*

Massachusetts
George Cobb *(Mt. Holyoke College, South Hadley)*; Cliff Kanold *(University of Massachusetts, Amherst)*

Michigan
Mary Bouck *(Farwell Area Schools)*; Carol Dorer *(Slauson Middle School, Ann Arbor)*; Carrie Heaney *(Forsythe Middle School, Ann Arbor)*; Ellen Hopkins *(Clague Middle School, Ann Arbor)*; Teri Keusch *(Portland Middle School, Portland)*; Valerie Mills *(Oakland Schools, Waterford)*; Mary Beth Schmitt *(Traverse City East Junior High, Traverse City)*; Jack Smith *(Michigan State University, East Lansing)*; Rebecca Spencer *(Sparta Middle School, Sparta)*; Ann Marie Nicoll Turner *(Tappan Middle School, Ann Arbor)*; Scott Turner *(Scarlett Middle School, Ann Arbor)*

Minnesota
Margarita Alvarez *(Olson Middle School, Minneapolis)*; Jane Amundson *(Nicollet Junior High, Burnsville)*; Anne Bartel *(Minneapolis Public Schools)*; Gwen Ranzau Campbell *(Sunrise Park Middle School, White Bear Lake)*; Stephanie Cin *(Hidden Valley Elementary, Burnsville)*; Joan Garfield *(University of Minnesota, Minneapolis)*; Gretchen Hall *(Richfield Middle School, Richfield)*; Jennifer Larson *(Olson Middle School, Minneapolis)*; Michele Luke *(West Junior High, Minnetonka)*; Jeni Meyer *(Richfield Junior High, Richfield)*; Judy Pfingsten *(Inver Grove Heights Middle School, Inver Grove Heights)*; Sarah Shafer *(North Junior High, Minnetonka)*; Genni Steele *(Central Middle School, White Bear Lake)*; Victoria Wilson *(Eisenhower Elementary, Hopkins)*; Paul Zorn *(St. Olaf College, Northfield)*

New York
Debra Altenau-Bartolino *(Greenwich Village Middle School, New York)*; Doug Clements *(University of Buffalo)*; Francis Curcio *(New York University, New York)*; Christine Dorosh *(Clinton School for Writers, Brooklyn)*; Jennifer Rehn *(East Side Middle School, New York)*; Phyllis Tam *(IS 89 Lab School, New York)*; Marie Turini *(Louis Armstrong Middle School, New York)*; Lucy West *(Community School District 2, New York)*; Monica Witt *(Simon Baruch Intermediate School 104, New York)*

Pennsylvania
Robert Aglietti *(Pittsburgh)*; Sharon Mihalich *(Pittsburgh)*; Jennifer Plumb *(South Hills Middle School, Pittsburgh)*; Mary Lynn Raith *(Pittsburgh Public Schools)*

Texas
Michelle Bittick *(Austin Independent School District)*; Margaret Cregg *(Plano Independent School District)*; Sheila Cunningham *(Klein Independent School District)*; Judy Hill *(Austin Independent School District)*; Patricia Holguin *(El Paso Independent School District)*; Bonnie McNemar *(Arlington)*; Kay Neuse *(Plano Independent School District)*; Joyce Polanco *(Austin Independent School District)*; Marge Ramirez *(University of Texas at El Paso)*; Pat Rossman *(Baker Campus, Austin)*; Cindy Schimek *(Houston)*; Cynthia Schneider *(Charles A. Dana Center, University of Texas at Austin)*; Uri Treisman *(Charles A. Dana Center, University of Texas at Austin)*; Jacqueline Weilmuenster *(Grapevine-Colleyville Independent School District)*; LuAnn Weynand *(San Antonio)*; Carmen Whitman *(Austin Independent School District)*; James Wohlgehagen *(Plano Independent School District)*

Washington
Ramesh Gangolli *(University of Washington, Seattle)*

Wisconsin
Susan Lamon *(Marquette University, Hales Corner)*; Steve Reinhart *(retired, Chippewa Falls Middle School, Eau Claire)*

Table of Contents

Samples and Populations
Data and Statistics

Samples and Populations

Data and Statistics

A radio talk-show host asked her listeners to call in to express their opinions about a local election. Could the results of this survey be used to describe the opinions of all the show's listeners?

Yung-nan takes 150 beans from a jar of beans, marks them with a red dot, and mixes them with the unmarked beans. Then she scoops out a few beans and counts the number of marked ones. Will this method help her predict the total number of beans in the jar?

How is it possible to estimate the deer population of a state, or even of a small part of the state?

The United States Census attempts to gather information from every household in the United States. Gathering, organizing, and analyzing data from such a large population is expensive and time-consuming. In most studies of large populations, data are gathered from a *sample*, or portion, of the population. The data from the sample are then used to make predictions or to draw conclusions about the full population.

Sampling is an important tool in statistics and data analysis. Understanding how to select samples and use them to make predictions will help you answer questions like those on the previous page.

Mathematical Highlights

Data and Statistics

In *Samples and Populations,* **you will explore ways of collecting and analyzing data.**

You will learn how to

- Use the process of statistical investigation to explore problems
- Use information from samples to draw conclusions about populations
- Explore the influence of sample size on the variability of the distribution of sample means or medians
- Evaluate sampling plans
- Use probability to select random samples from populations
- Compare sample distributions using measures of center (mean, median), measures of variability (range, minimum and maximum data values, percentiles), and displays that group data (histograms, box-and-whisker plots)
- Explore relationships between paired values of numerical variables

As you work on the problems in this unit, ask yourself questions about situations that involve analyzing data using samples.

What is the population?

What is the sample?

What kinds of comparisons and relationships can I explore using data from the sample?

Can I use my results to make predictions or generalizations about the population?

Investigation 1

Comparing Data Sets

American shoppers have a great variety of products from which to choose. Many people turn to information in consumer surveys and product comparisons to help make decisions.

A consumer magazine rated 37 varieties of peanut butter. Each peanut butter was assigned a quality rating from 1 to 100 points. A panel of trained tasters made two general statements about quality:

- Peanut butters with higher quality ratings were smooth; had a sweet, nutty flavor; and were not overly dry or sticky.

- Peanut butters with lower quality ratings were not very nutty, had small bits of peanuts, or had a burnt or slightly rancid taste.

The article also gave the sodium content and price per 3-tablespoon serving for each type. Peanut butters were classified according to three attributes: natural or regular, creamy or chunky, and salted or unsalted. The data are presented in the table on the next page. A fourth attribute, name brand or store brand, has been added to the data.

Peanut Butter Comparison

	Peanut Butter	Quality Rating	Sodium per Serving (mg)	Price per Serving (cents)	Regular/ Natural	Creamy/ Chunky	Salted/ Unsalted	Name Brand/ Store Brand
1.	Smucker's Natural	71	15	27	natural	creamy	unsalted	name
2.	Deaf Smith Arrowhead	69	0	32	natural	creamy	unsalted	name
3.	Adams 100% Natural	60	0	26	natural	creamy	unsalted	name
4.	Adams	60	168	26	natural	creamy	salted	name
5.	Laura Scudder's All Natural	57	165	26	natural	creamy	salted	name
6.	Country Pure Brand	52	225	21	natural	creamy	salted	store
7.	Hollywood Natural	34	15	32	natural	creamy	unsalted	name
8.	Smucker's Natural	89	15	27	natural	chunky	unsalted	name
9.	Adams 100% Natural	69	0	26	natural	chunky	unsalted	name
10.	Deaf Smith Arrowhead	69	0	32	natural	chunky	unsalted	name
11.	Country Pure Brand	67	105	21	natural	chunky	salted	store
12.	Laura Scudder's All Natural	63	165	24	natural	chunky	salted	name
13.	Smucker's Natural	57	188	26	natural	chunky	salted	name
14.	Health Valley 100%	40	3	34	natural	chunky	unsalted	name
15.	Jif	76	220	22	regular	creamy	salted	name
16.	Skippy	60	225	19	regular	creamy	salted	name
17.	Kroger	54	240	14	regular	creamy	salted	store
18.	NuMade	43	187	20	regular	creamy	salted	store
19.	Peter Pan	40	225	21	regular	creamy	salted	name
20.	Peter Pan	35	3	22	regular	creamy	unsalted	name
21.	A & P	34	225	12	regular	creamy	salted	store
22.	Food Club	33	225	17	regular	creamy	salted	store
23.	Pathmark	31	255	9	regular	creamy	salted	store
24.	Lady Lee	23	225	16	regular	creamy	salted	store
25.	Albertsons	23	225	17	regular	creamy	salted	store
26.	ShurFine	11	225	16	regular	creamy	salted	store
27.	Jif	83	162	23	regular	chunky	salted	name
28.	Skippy	83	211	21	regular	chunky	salted	name
29.	Food Club	54	195	17	regular	chunky	salted	store
30.	Kroger	49	255	14	regular	chunky	salted	store
31.	A & P	46	225	11	regular	chunky	salted	store
32.	Peter Pan	45	180	22	regular	chunky	salted	name
33.	NuMade	40	208	21	regular	chunky	salted	store
34.	Lady Lee	34	225	16	regular	chunky	salted	store
35.	Albertsons	31	225	17	regular	chunky	salted	store
36.	Pathmark	29	210	9	regular	chunky	salted	store
37.	ShurFine	26	195	16	regular	chunky	salted	store

SOURCE: *Consumer Reports* and *Workshop Statistics: Student Activity Guide*

Getting Ready for Problem 1.1

- Who might be interested in the results of this peanut butter study?
- What questions about peanut butter can be answered with these data?
- What questions about peanut butter cannot be answered with these data?

1.1 From Line Plots to Histograms

In this problem, you will look at the **distribution** of quality ratings for the regular peanut butters. You will use measures of center, minimum and maximum values, range, the shape of the data, and where the data cluster to describe the distribution. Locate quality ratings in the table.

Did You Know?

Arachibutyrophobia (uh rak ih byoo tih ruh FOH bee uh) is the fear of getting peanut butter stuck to the roof of your mouth!

A. Each dot on the line plot below represents the quality rating of one regular peanut butter from the table.

Regular Peanut Butter Quality Ratings

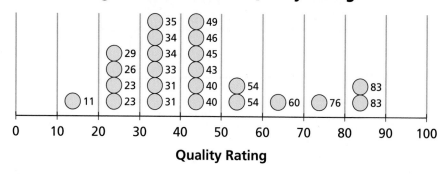

Quality Rating

1. Which interval (or intervals) includes the most quality ratings?

2. Look at the interval marked 40 to 50. What is the lowest rating in this interval? What is the highest rating in this interval?

3. Suppose you want to add a quality rating of 50 to the plot. In which interval would you put this value? Explain.

4. Suppose you want to add a quality rating of 59. In which interval would you put this value? Explain.

5. What do you think is the typical rating for regular peanut butters? Explain.

B. In the plot below, the collection of dots in the intervals have been used to make bars that show the number of data values in each interval.

Regular Peanut Butter Quality Ratings

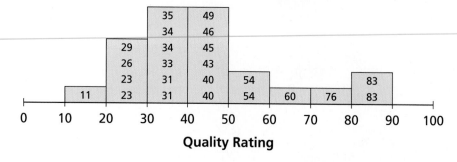

Quality Rating

1. To which interval would you add each of these quality ratings: 93, 69, 10, and 57?

2. How would you change the bar in an interval to show the addition of a new quality rating?

For: Stat Tools
Visit: PHSchool.com
Web Code: apd-8101

C. The **histogram** below shows the same distribution as the interval bars with numerical values in Question B. A frequency axis has been added to the side of the plot.

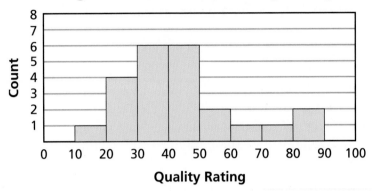

Regular Peanut Butter Quality Ratings

1. How is this histogram the same as the plot in Question B? How is it different?

2. Why is a scale on the vertical axis needed? What information does the scale provide?

3. To which interval would you add each of these quality ratings: 93, 69, 10, and 57? How would you change each bar to show a new quality rating?

D. Describe the distribution of quality ratings for the regular peanut butters. Use information from both the histogram and the table. Include the following in your description:

● the minimum and maximum values

● the range of the data and any outliers

● intervals where data cluster

● the shape of the distribution

● related statistics, such as the mean and median

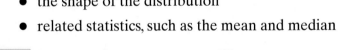
ACE Homework starts on page 17.

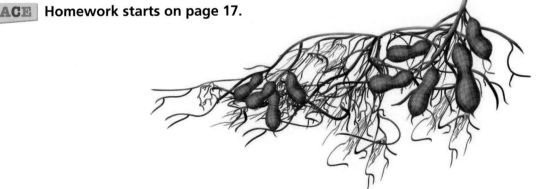

1.2 Using Histograms

In this problem, you will consider quality ratings for the natural peanut butters, which have no preservatives. By comparing histograms, you can decide whether natural or regular peanut butters have higher quality ratings.

Getting Ready for Problem

This list summarizes how to examine and describe a data distribution.

- *Read the data.* Identify individual values, the minimum and maximum data values, and the range.
- *Read between the data.* Identify intervals where the data cluster or there are gaps in the data.
- *Read beyond the data.* Describe the shape of the distribution. Identify statistics, such as the mean and median, and relate them to the shape of the distribution.

Look back at the way you described the distribution of quality ratings in Problem 1.1. Did you consider all the things mentioned above?

Problem 1.2 Using Histograms

A. 1. Make a histogram of the quality ratings for natural peanut butters. Use 10-point interval widths.

2. Describe the distribution of quality ratings.

B. 1. The histogram in Problem 1.1 shows the quality ratings for the regular peanut butters. The interval width is 10 quality points. Make a new histogram of the quality ratings for regular peanut butters. This time, use interval widths of 5.

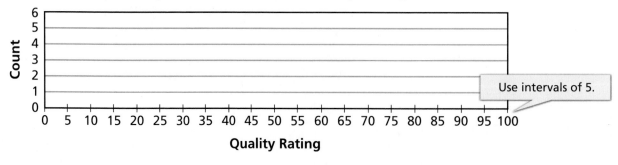

Regular Peanut Butter Quality Ratings

Use intervals of 5.

2. Make another histogram of the same data. Use interval widths of either 2 or 15.

3. a. Compare the histogram from Problem 1.1 and the histograms you made in parts (1) and (2). What is the same about the three histograms? What is different?

    b. What are the reasons for the differences in the histograms?

    c. Would your decision about what is a typical quality rating be affected by the histogram you used? Explain.

4. This rule of thumb can help you choose a good interval width for a histogram:

If possible, use a width that gives 8–10 bars.

Using this rule of thumb, which of the three histograms is best for representing the distribution of quality ratings for the regular peanut butters?

C. When the data sets you want to compare have different numbers of entries, you can change the vertical axis to show the percent of all values that lie in each interval. This is called a *relative frequency histogram*.

    1. Make two new histograms like the one started below, one for natural peanut butters and one for regular peanut butters. Because 1 out of 14 of the natural peanut butters has a quality rating between 80 and 90 points, the relative frequency for this interval is 7%.

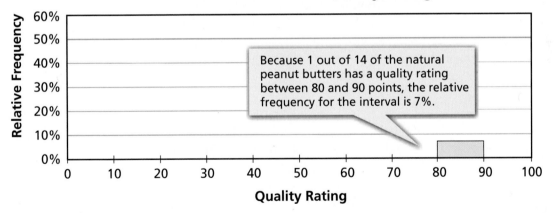

Natural Peanut Butter Quality Ratings

Because 1 out of 14 of the natural peanut butters has a quality rating between 80 and 90 points, the relative frequency for the interval is 7%.

    2. Do natural peanut butters or regular peanut butters have higher quality ratings? Use the histograms and other relevant information to justify your choice.

ACE Homework starts on page 17.

Box-and-whisker plots, or *box plots*, are useful for showing the distribution of values in a data set. The box plot below is an example.

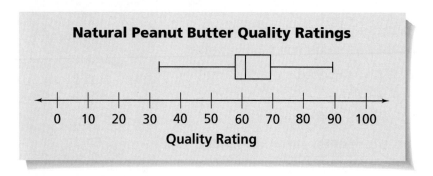

A box plot is constructed from the **five-number summary** of the data, which includes the minimum value, maximum value, median, lower quartile, and upper quartile.

When a set of data is ordered from least to greatest, the **lower quartile** is the median of the values to the left of the median. The **upper quartile** is the median of the values to the right of the median.

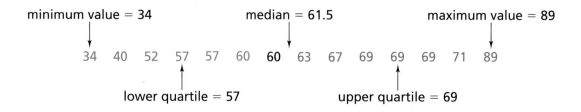

The box plot below shows how the five-number summary corresponds to the features of the box plot.

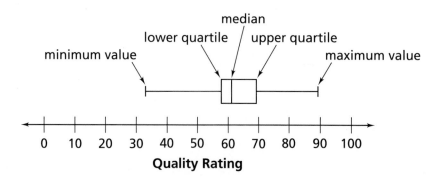

The five-number summary divides a data distribution into four parts.

About what percent of the data values fall in each of the following intervals?

- before the median
- after the median
- in the box (between the upper and lower quartiles)
- before the upper quartile
- after the upper quartile
- before the lower quartile
- after the lower quartile
- between the median and the upper quartile
- between the median and the lower quartile

What do you think the term *quartile* means?

You can compare distributions by displaying two or more box plots on the same scale.

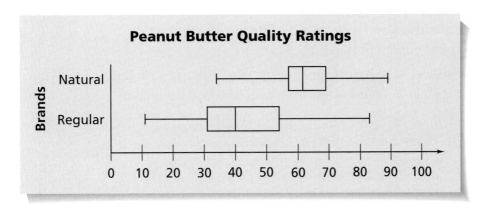

Many people consider *both* quality and price when deciding which products to buy. The box plots at the right show the distributions of per-serving prices for natural peanut butters and regular peanut butters.

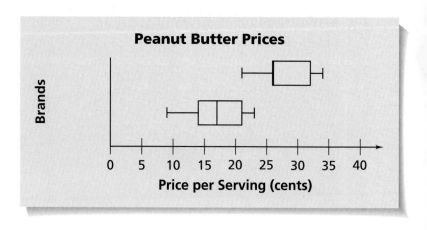

Peanut Butter Prices

Brands

Price per Serving (cents)

Problem 1.3 Box-and-Whisker Plots

In the Peanut Butter Comparisons table (before Problem 1.1), refer to the column that gives the price per serving.

A. 1. Calculate the five-number summary for the prices of the natural peanut butters.

 2. Calculate the five-number summary for the prices of the regular peanut butters.

 3. Which box plot above represents the distribution of prices for natural peanut butters and which represents the distribution of prices for regular peanut butters?

 4. How do the prices of the natural peanut butters compare with the prices of the regular peanut butters? Explain how you can make this comparison using box plots.

B. Refer to the plots below and the plots in Question A.

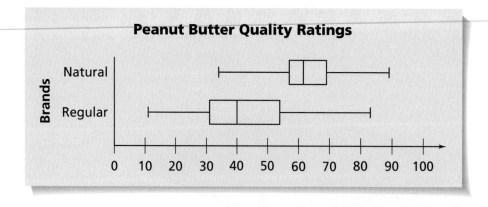

Peanut Butter Quality Ratings

Brands

Natural

Regular

 1. Suppose price is the only factor a buyer considers. Is natural peanut butter or regular peanut butter a better choice? Explain.

 2. Suppose quality is the only factor a buyer considers. Is natural peanut butter or regular peanut butter a better choice?

C. In a box plot, the length of the box represents the difference between the upper and lower quartiles. The difference is called the *interquartile range* (IQR).

1. What is the IQR for the quality ratings for natural peanut butters? What does it tell you?

2. What is the IQR for the quality ratings for regular peanut butters? What does it tell you?

D. Values in a data set that are much greater or much less than most of the other values are called *outliers*. To decide whether a value is an outlier, first find the IQR. Outliers are data values that are either

• greater than 1.5 times the IQR added to the upper quartile, or

• less than 1.5 times the IQR subtracted from the lower quartile

1. What are the outliers in the quality ratings for the natural peanut butters?

2. What are the outliers in the ratings for the regular peanut butters?

3. On a box plot, outliers are sometimes indicated with asterisks (*). The box plots in Question B and the box plots below show the same data distributions.

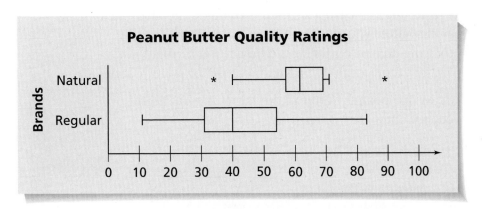

a. In the Question B plots, the whiskers extend to the minimum and maximum values. What values do the whiskers in the plots above extend to?

b. Describe how you would construct a box plot if you wanted to show the outliers in the distribution.

E. 1. Make a pair of box plots to compare the quality ratings for creamy and chunky peanut butters.

2. What is the IQR for each distribution? Use the IQR to determine whether there are any outliers.

3. Based on quality ratings, are creamy peanut butters or chunky peanut butters a better choice? Explain.

ACE Homework starts on page 17.

1.4 Making a Quality Choice

In this problem, you will use what you have learned to compare quality ratings for salted and unsalted peanut butters and for name brand and store brand peanut butters.

Problem 1.4 Analyzing Data

Justify your answers to the following questions with statistics and graphs, such as histograms and box plots.

A. Compare the quality ratings of salted peanut butters with the quality ratings of unsalted peanut butters. Based on quality ratings, are salted peanut butters or unsalted peanut butters a better choice?

B. Compare the quality ratings of name brands with the quality ratings of store brands. Based on quality ratings, are name brands or store brands a better choice?

C. Use your results from this and earlier problems to name the attributes of the type of peanut butter you would recommend to someone. Be sure to say whether the peanut butter would be natural or regular, creamy or chunky, salted or unsalted, and name brand or store brand.

D. Can you find at least one peanut butter in the table that has all the attributes you recommend?

ACE **Homework starts on page 17.**

Applications

1. The horizontal scale of a histogram begins at 40 and has interval widths of 10. In which intervals are the values 85 and 90 located?

2. **a.** Make two histograms, using the Peanut Butter Comparisons table before Problem 1.1, that allow you to compare the prices of natural peanut butters with the prices of regular peanut butters.

   b. What interval widths did you use? Why?

   c. Did you show counts or percents on the vertical axis? Why?

For Exercises 3–5, refer to the Peanut Butter Comparisons table. Use statistics and histograms to justify each answer.

3. Based on price, are creamy peanut butters or chunky peanut butters a better choice?

4. Based on price, are salted peanut butters or unsalted peanut butters a better choice?

5. Based on price, are name brands or store brands a better choice?

6. **a.** Suppose someone wants to choose a peanut butter based on price. Use your answers for Exercises 2–5 to list the four attributes— natural or regular, creamy or chunky, salted or unsalted, and name brand or store brand—you would recommend.

   b. Can you find at least one type of peanut butter that has all the attributes you recommend?

Use the histograms and box plots below for Exercises 7–17.

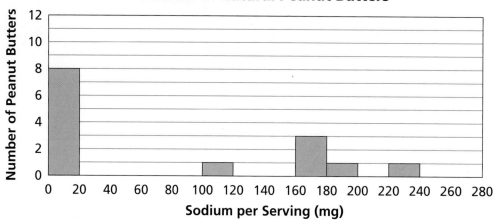

Sodium in Natural Peanut Butters

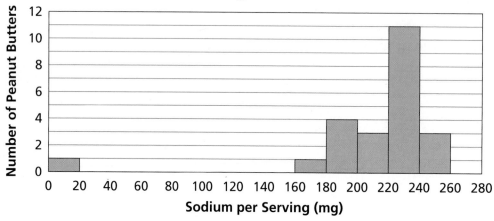

Sodium in Regular Peanut Butters

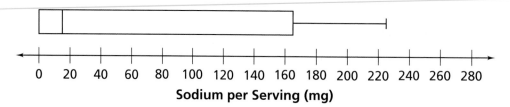

Box Plot A

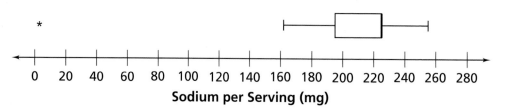

Box Plot B

7. Which box plot shows the distribution of sodium values for the natural peanut butters? Explain.

8. Which box plot shows the distribution of sodium values for the regular peanut butters? Explain.

9. What is the median of the sodium values for the natural peanut butters? Explain what this tells you.

10. What is the median of the sodium values for the regular peanut butters? Explain what this tells you.

11. Where do the sodium values for natural peanut butters cluster?

12. Where do the sodium values for regular peanut butters cluster?

13. Suppose you are on a low sodium diet. Should you choose a regular or natural peanut butter? Explain.

For Exercises 14 and 15, fill in the blanks.

14. The sodium values for the natural peanut butters vary from ⟶?⟶ to ⟶?⟶. The range is ⟶?⟶.

15. The sodium values for the regular peanut butters vary from ⟶?⟶ to ⟶?⟶. The range is ⟶?⟶.

16. Box Plot A is missing a "whisker." Explain why.

17. Use the IQR to help you identify which data values are outliers in the sodium values for the regular peanut butters shown on Box Plot B.

18. **Multiple Choice** Which value is *not* needed to construct a box plot?

　A. upper quartile　　　**B.** minimum value

　C. median　　　　　　**D.** mean

Use the histograms below for Exercises 19–21. The means and medians are marked on each histogram.

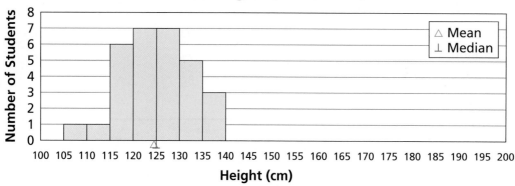

Student Heights (Grades K–2)

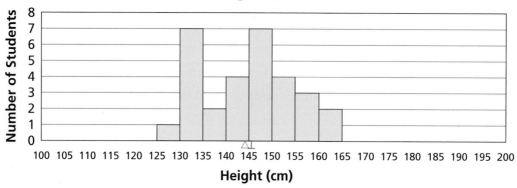

Student Heights (Grades 3–5)

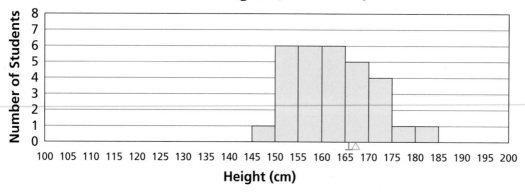

Student Heights (Grades 6–8)

19. How much taller is a student in grades 6–8 than a student in grades K–2? Explain.

20. How much taller is a student in grades 6–8 than a student in grades 3–5?

21. The heights for the students in grades 3–5 cluster in a different way than those for students in grades K–2 and 6–8. What is different about the heights for the students in grades 3–5? Why do you think this might be so?

The graphs below compare prices (in U.S. dollars) of juice drinks sold in the United Kingdom. The titles and axis labels are missing. Use the graphs for Exercises 22–25.

Graph B

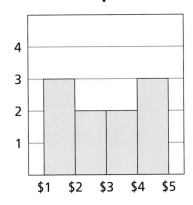

Graph A

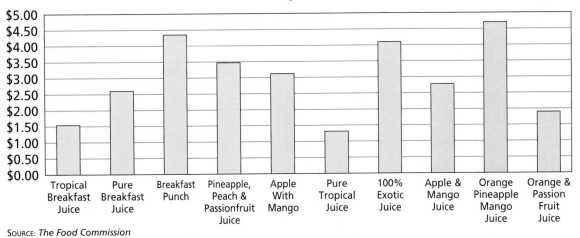

SOURCE: *The Food Commission*

22. Which graph could you use to identify the juice drinks with the greatest and least prices? Give the names of these drinks and their estimated prices.

23. What title and axis labels would be appropriate for each graph?

24. Suppose you were given only Graph A. Would you have enough information to make Graph B? Explain.

25. Suppose you were given only Graph B. Would you have enough information to make Graph A? Explain.

26. Tim says TastiSnak raisins are a better deal than Harvest Time raisins because there are more raisins in each box. Kadisha says that, because a box of either type contains half an ounce, both brands give you the same amount for your money.

The students found the number of raisins and the mass for 50 boxes of each type. They made the plots below. Based on this information, which brand is a better deal? Explain.

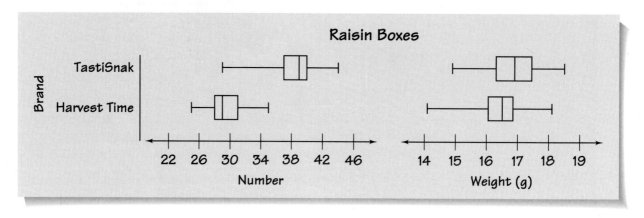

Connections

27. a. Make a data set with 20 values and a mean of 25.

   b. Do you think other students made the same data set as you? Explain.

   c. Does the median of the data set need to be close in value to the mean? Explain.

28. a. Some students were asked to randomly choose a number from 1 to 10. The results are shown. Make a circle graph of these data.

For: Multiple-Choice Skills Practice
Web Code: apa-8154

Random Number Choosing

Number	1	2	3	4	5	6	7	8	9	10
Percent of Students Who Chose Number	1	5	12	11	10	12	30	9	7	3

   b. Make a bar graph of these data.

   c. What is the mode of the numbers selected?

   d. Based on the results, do you think the students actually chose the numbers at random?

   e. Nine students chose 5 as their number. How many students are in the seventh grade?

29. At a diving competition, Jeff's dive receives seven scores with a mean of 9.0. For his final score, the greatest and least scores are removed and the mean of the remaining scores is calculated. Jeff's final score for the dive is 9.1. What is the sum of the two removed scores? Explain.

30. Use the tables from National Basketball Association (NBA) teams below, statistics, and graphs to justify your answers to parts (a)–(c).

2004 Houston Rockets

Player	Age	Height (cm)
Baker	34	211
Barry	36	196
Bowen	30	206
Braggs	29	203
Howard	32	206
McGrady	26	203
Mutombo	39	218
Norris	32	185
Padgett	29	206
Sura	32	196
Ward	35	188
Weatherspoon	35	200
Wesley	35	185
Yao	25	229

SOURCE: *www.nba.com*

2004 Chicago Bulls

Player	Age	Height (cm)
Chandler	23	216
Curry	23	211
Davis	37	206
Deng	20	203
Duhon	23	185
Gordon	22	191
Griffin	31	196
Harrington	31	206
Hinrich	24	191
Nocioni	26	200
Pargo	26	185
Piatowski	35	200
Reiner	23	211
Williams	25	191

SOURCE: *www.nba.com*

   a. Are the players on one team older than the players on the other team, or are they about the same age?

   b. Are the players on one team taller than the players on the other team, or are they about the same height?

   c. Based on these data, what estimates would you make for the age and height distributions of a typical professional men's basketball team? What cautions would you suggest in making generalizations from the given data?

31. Vicky has misplaced one of her algebra quizzes. The scores on the quizzes she has are 82, 71, 83, 91, and 78. She knows that the mean of all six quiz scores is 79.5. What is the score on the missing quiz?

32. Terrence's test scores in math class this semester are 98, 83, 72, 85, 91, 79, and 85. He thinks he can reasonably expect an 87 or better average for his semester grade. Without doing an exact computation, do you think he is correct? Explain.

Extensions

33. Bill and Joe are interested in baseball. The histogram below shows data they collected about the duration of baseball games. The title and axes labels are missing.

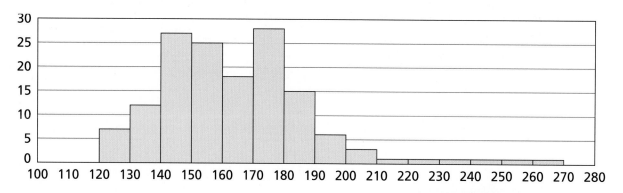

a. What title and axis labels are appropriate for this graph?

b. What does the shape of the graph tell you about the length of a typical baseball game?

c. About how many games are represented in the graph?

d. Estimate the lower quartile, median, and upper quartile for these data. What do these numbers tell you about the length of a typical baseball game?

Mathematical Reflections 1

In this investigation, you grouped data into intervals to make histograms, and you used the five-number summaries of data sets to make box plots. You used these graphs to analyze and compare data distributions. These questions will help you summarize what you have learned.

Think about your answers to these questions. Discuss your ideas with other students and your teacher. Then write a summary of your findings in your notebook.

1. **a.** Describe how to construct a histogram for a set of data.

   b. Describe how to construct a box plot for a set of data.

   c. In what ways are histograms and box plots alike? In what ways are they different?

2. **a.** How can you compare two data sets displayed in histograms?

   b. How can you compare two data sets displayed in box plots?

Choosing a Sample From a Population

Suppose you want to gather information about students in your class, such as their preferences for food, television, music, or sports. It would be fairly easy to conduct a survey. But collecting information about all the students in your school or all the people in your city, your state, or the entire country would be very difficult.

You can study a large population by collecting data from a small part, or **sample,** of that population. Depending on how the sample is selected from the population, it is possible to use data from the sample to help you *make predictions* or *draw conclusions* about the entire population. The challenge is to choose a sample that is likely to help you accurately predict information about a population.

Consider this information.

- The average child eats 1,500 peanut butter and jelly sandwiches before graduating from high school.

- Between grades 7 and 12, teenagers listen to about 10,500 hours of rock music. This is only 500 fewer hours than they spend in school over 12 years.

- The average American child watches 30,000 commercials each year.

How could the groups who reported these data know about the activities of all the children or teenagers in the United States?

Do you think each of these facts was gathered from a census (a survey of every person in the population) or from a sample?

Newspapers, magazines, radio and television programs, and Internet sites conduct surveys on a variety of subjects. Suppose a magazine with a national circulation asked its readers the five questions about honesty shown below. The magazine asks the readers to go to their Web site and enter their answers.

HONESTY SURVEY

1. **What would you do if you found someone's wallet on the street?**

   a. Try to return it to the owner
   b. Return it, but keep the money
   c. Keep the wallet and the money

2. **What would you do if a cashier mistakenly gave you $10 extra in change?**

   a. Tell the cashier about the error
   b. Say nothing and keep the cash

3. **Would you cheat on an exam if you were sure you wouldn't get caught?**

   a. Yes
   b. No

4. **Would you download music from the Internet illegally instead of buying the CD?**

   a. Yes
   b. No

5. **Do you feel that you are an honest person in most situations?**

   a. Yes
   b. No

Problem 2.1 Using a Sample to Make Predictions

A. A *sampling plan* is a strategy for choosing a sample from a population. What is the population for the honesty survey? What is the sample? How is the sample chosen from the population?

B. Suppose 5,280 people complete the survey, and 4,224 of them answer "No" to Question 3. What percent of responders said they would not cheat on an exam?

C. Of the 5,280 responders, 1,584 answer yes to Question 4. What percent of responders said they would not download music illegally from the Internet?

D. Refer to the survey results given in Questions B and C. The United States population is about 300 million.

    1. Estimate how many people in the United States would say they would not cheat on an exam.

    2. Estimate how many people in the United States would say they would not download music illegally from the Internet.

E. List some reasons why predictions about all Americans based on this survey might be inaccurate.

F. How could you revise the sampling plan for this survey so you would be more confident that the results predict the percent of the United States population that is honest?

ACE Homework starts on page 36.

2.2 Selecting a Sample

Making accurate predictions about a population based on a sample can be complicated, even when you are interested in a relatively small population.

Suppose you are doing research on the lives of students at your school. You would like to answer these questions:

- How many hours of sleep do students get each night?
- How many movies do students watch each week?

If your school has a large student population, it might be difficult to gather and analyze data from every student.

How could you select a sample of your school population to survey?

Problem 2.2 Selecting a Sample

Ms. Ruiz's class wants to conduct this survey about hours spent sleeping and watching movies. They plan to survey students in their school. The class divides into four groups. Each group devises a plan for sampling the school population.

- Each member of Group 1 will survey the students who ride on his or her school bus.

- Group 2 will survey every fourth person in the cafeteria line.

- Group 3 will post a notice in the morning announcements asking for volunteers for their survey.

- Group 4 will randomly select 30 students for their survey from a list of three-digit student ID numbers. They will label the faces of a 10-sided solid with the numbers 0 through 9 and roll it three times to generate each number.

A. What are the advantages and disadvantages of each sampling plan?

B. Which plan do you think will lead to the most accurate predictions for students in the whole school? Explain.

C. The four sampling plans are examples of common sampling methods.

1. Group 1's plan is an example of **convenience sampling.** What do you think convenience sampling is? Describe another plan that would use convenience sampling.

2. Group 2's plan is an example of **systematic sampling.** What do you think systematic sampling is? Describe another plan that would use systematic sampling.

3. Group 3's plan is an example of **voluntary-response sampling.** What do you think voluntary-response sampling is? Describe another plan that would use voluntary-response sampling.

4. Group 4's plan is an example of **random sampling.** What do you think random sampling is? Describe another plan that would use random sampling.

D. Jahmal thinks Group 1's and Group 3's plans may not give samples that are likely to predict what is typical of the population. Do you agree or disagree? Explain.

ACE Homework starts on page 36.

2.3 Choosing Random Samples

In most cases, a good sampling plan is one that gives each sample selected from the population the same chance of being chosen. Sampling plans with this property are called random sampling plans. Samples chosen with a random sampling plan are called random samples.

To select a random sample from a population of 100 students, you could use spinners like these to generate pairs of random digits.

What two-digit numbers can you generate with these spinners?

How can you make sure student 100 has an equally likely chance of being included in your sample?

There are many other ways to select a random sample of students. For example, you could roll two 10-sided solids or generate random numbers with your calculator.

Getting Ready for Problem

Suppose you have two concert tickets. You want to choose one of your six best friends to go with you. Consider these possible strategies:

Strategy 1: Choose the first person who calls you tonight.

Strategy 2: Assign each friend a different whole number from 1 to 6. The number you roll on a six-sided number cube determines who goes.

Strategy 3: Tell each friend to meet you after school. Toss a coin to choose between the first two friends who arrive.

- You want to give each friend the same chance of being selected. Which strategy would accomplish this? Explain.

- Describe another strategy that would give each of your friends an equally likely chance of being selected.

The table on the next page shows data collected on a Monday in an eighth-grade class. The data include the number of hours of sleep each student got the previous night and the number of movies each student watched the previous week.

You can use statistics about a random sample of these data to make predictions about the entire population.

Problem 2.3 Choosing Random Samples

You are going to choose a sample and represent your sample with a line plot and a box plot. To make it easier to compare your sample's distribution with others, your class should decide on a scale before starting.

A. 1. Use spinners, 10-sided number cubes, a graphing calculator, or some other method to select a random sample of 30 students. (Your sample should contain 30 *different* students. If you select a student who is already in your sample, select another.)

    2. For each student in your sample, record the number of movies watched and the number of hours slept.

B. 1. Make a line plot showing the distribution of the movie data from your sample.

    2. Describe the variability in the number of movies watched by students in your sample.

    3. Compare your distribution with those of other members of your class. Describe any similarities or differences.

    4. What can you conclude about the movie-watching behavior of the population of 100 students based on all the samples? Explain.

C. 1. Make a box plot showing the distributions of the hours of sleep from your sample.

    2. Describe the variability in the number of hours of sleep for students in your sample.

    3. Compare your distribution with those of the other members of your class. Describe any similarities or differences.

    4. What can you conclude about the hours of sleep of the population of 100 students based on the samples selected by members of your class? Explain.

ACE Homework starts on page 36.

Grade 8 Database

Student Number	Gender	Sleep (h)	Movies
01	boy	11.5	14
02	boy	2.0	8
03	girl	7.7	3
04	boy	9.3	1
05	boy	7.1	16
06	boy	7.5	1
07	boy	8.0	4
08	girl	7.8	1
09	girl	8.0	13
10	girl	8.0	15
11	boy	9.0	1
12	boy	9.2	10
13	boy	8.5	5
14	girl	6.0	15
15	boy	6.5	10
16	boy	8.3	2
17	girl	7.4	2
18	boy	11.2	3
19	girl	7.3	1
20	boy	8.0	0
21	girl	7.8	1
22	girl	7.8	1
23	boy	9.2	2
24	girl	7.5	0
25	boy	8.8	1
26	girl	8.5	0
27	girl	9.0	0
28	girl	8.5	0
29	boy	8.2	2
30	girl	7.8	2
31	girl	8.0	2
32	girl	7.3	8
33	boy	6.0	5
34	girl	7.5	5
35	boy	6.5	5
36	boy	9.3	1
37	girl	8.2	3
38	boy	7.3	3
39	girl	7.4	6
40	girl	8.5	7
41	boy	5.5	17
42	boy	6.5	3
43	boy	7.0	5
44	girl	8.5	2
45	girl	9.3	4
46	girl	8.0	15
47	boy	8.5	10
48	girl	6.2	11
49	girl	11.8	10
50	girl	9.0	4

Student Number	Gender	Sleep (h)	Movies
51	boy	5.0	4
52	boy	6.5	5
53	girl	8.5	2
54	boy	9.1	15
55	girl	7.5	2
56	girl	8.5	1
57	girl	8.0	2
58	girl	7.0	7
59	girl	8.4	10
60	girl	9.5	1
61	girl	7.3	5
62	girl	7.3	4
63	boy	8.5	3
64	boy	9.0	3
65	boy	9.0	4
66	girl	7.3	5
67	girl	5.7	0
68	girl	5.5	0
69	boy	10.5	7
70	girl	7.5	1
71	boy	7.8	0
72	girl	7.3	1
73	boy	9.3	2
74	boy	9.0	1
75	boy	8.7	1
76	boy	8.5	3
77	girl	9.0	1
78	boy	8.0	1
79	boy	8.0	4
80	boy	6.5	0
81	boy	8.0	0
82	girl	9.0	8
83	girl	8.0	0
84	boy	7.0	0
85	boy	9.0	6
86	boy	7.3	0
87	Gender / girl	9.0	3
88	girl	7.5	5
89	boy	8.0	0
90	girl	7.5	6
91	boy	8.0	4
92	boy	9.0	4
93	boy	7.0	0
94	boy	8.0	3
95	boy	8.3	3
96	boy	8.3	14
97	girl	7.8	5
98	girl	8.5	1
99	girl	8.3	3
100	boy	7.5	2

2.4 Choosing a Sample Size

In Problem 2.3, you used random samples to estimate the sleep and movie-viewing habits of 100 students.

Could you make good estimates with less work by selecting smaller samples?

In this problem, you will explore how the size of a sample affects the accuracy of statistical estimates.

Problem 2.4 Choosing a Sample Size

A. From the population of 100 students in Problem 2.3, select a random sample of 5 students and a random sample of 10 students. Record the number of movies watched and number of hours slept for each student. (The students *within* each sample should be different, but the same student may appear in both samples.)

B. 1. Use the samples in Question A and the sample of 30 students from Problem 2.3. For each sample, find the mean and median number of movies watched and the mean and median number of hours of sleep.

2. Record the means and the medians in a class chart. This chart will contain means and medians from everyone's samples.

C. 1. Use the class data about the mean number of movies watched. For each sample size (samples of 5, 10, and 30 students), make a line plot of the distribution of the means. You will have three line plots. Compare the three distributions. Describe the variability in each distribution.

2. The mean number of movies watched for the entire population of 100 students is about 4. Write a paragraph describing how well the means for samples of different sizes predict the mean for the population.

D. 1. Use the class data about the median number of movies watched. For each sample size, make a line plot of the distribution of the medians. You will have three line plots. Compare the three distributions. Describe the variability in each distribution.

2. The median number of movies watched for all 100 students is 3. Write a paragraph describing how well the medians for samples of different sizes predict the median for the population.

E. For the entire population, the mean number of hours slept is 7.7, and the median is 10. Follow the procedures you used in Questions C and D to explore the distribution of means and medians for the samples of different sizes. Discuss how well samples of different sizes predict the mean and median for the entire population.

F. Suppose each student in your class chose a sample of 50 students and found the mean and median of the data for movies watched and hours slept. What would you expect line plots of these means and medians to look like? Explain.

ACE **Homework starts on page 36.**

Applications

For Exercises 1–4, describe the population and the sampling method.

1. A magazine for teenagers asks its readers to write in with information about how they solve personal problems.

2. An eighth-grade class wants to find out how much time middle school students spend on the telephone each day. Students in the class keep a record of the amount of time they spend on the phone each day for a week.

3. Ms. Darnell's class wants to estimate the number of soft drinks middle school students drink each day. They obtain a list of students in the school and write each name on a card. They put the cards in a box and select the names of 40 students to survey.

4. A survey found that 52% of American adults believe that global warming is a serious threat. The editors of the school paper want to find out how students in their school feel about this issue. They select 26 students for their survey—one whose name begins with A, one whose name begins with B, one whose name begins with C, and so on.

A middle school has 350 students. One math class wants to find out how many hours a typical student in the school spent doing homework last week. Several students suggest sampling plans. For Exercises 5–8, name the type of sampling method and tell whether you think it would give a sample that lets you make accurate predictions about the population.

5. Zak suggests surveying every third student on each homeroom class list.

6. Kwang-Hee suggests putting 320 white beans and 30 red beans in a bag. Each student would draw a bean as he or she enters the auditorium for tomorrow's assembly. The 30 students who draw red beans will be surveyed.

7. Ushio suggests that each student in the class survey everyone in his or her English class.

8. Kirby suggests putting surveys on a table at the entrance to the school and asking students to return completed questionnaires at the end of the day.

9. A radio host asked her listeners to call in to express their opinions about a local election. What kind of sampling method is she using? Do you think the results of this survey could be used to describe the opinions of all the show's listeners? Explain.

Manufacturers often conduct quality-control tests on samples of their products. For Exercises 10–13, describe a random sampling plan you would recommend to the company. Justify your recommendation.

10. A toy company produces 5,000 video-game systems each day.

11. A music company manufactures a total of 200,000 compact discs for about 100 recording artists each day.

12. A fireworks company produces more than 1,500 rockets each day.

13. A bottling company produces 25,000 bottles of spring water each day.

14. a. In Problem 2.3, suppose that, instead of choosing random samples of 30 students, you select the first 30 students for your sample, a second student selects the next 30 students for his sample, and so on. Is this procedure likely to result in samples that allow you to make accurate predictions about the population?

  b. Suppose you select students 1, 5, 9, 13, 17, 21, 25, . . . for your sample. Is this sample likely to allow you to make accurate predictions about the population?

For: Help with Exercise 14
Web Code: ape-8214

15. a. The homecoming committee wants to estimate how many students will attend the homecoming dance. However, they don't want to ask every student in the school. Describe a method the committee could use to select a sample of students to survey.

b. Describe how the committee could use the results of its survey to predict the number of students who will attend the dance.

For Exercises 16 and 17, use the graph below.

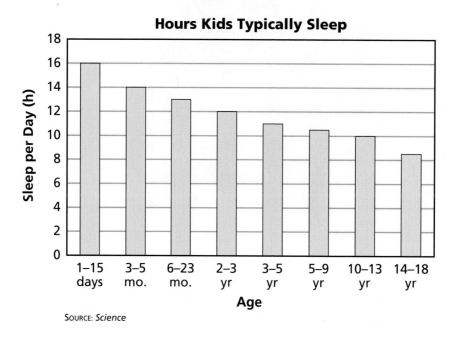

SOURCE: *Science*

16. About how many more hours per day does a newborn sleep than a typical 10- to 13-year-old?

17. Suppose you want to survey a random sample of students in your school to find out how many hours they sleep each night. Which would be the best sample size: 5 students, 10 students, or 30 students? Explain.

Connections

18. Multiple Choice This stem-and-leaf plot shows Ella's diving scores from a recent competition. What was Ella's lowest score for the competition?

A. 0.03 **B.** 1.4

C. 8.0 **D.** None of these

Ella's Diving Scores

5	1 4
6	1
7	6
8	0 3

Key: 5 | 1 means 5.1

19. a. From age 5–18, the average student eats 1,500 peanut butter and jelly sandwiches. You can make about 15 sandwiches from an 18-ounce jar of peanut butter. How many jars of peanut butter would you need to make 1,500 sandwiches? Explain.

   b. About how many jars of peanut butter does an average student eat each year from age 5 to age 18?

   c. How many peanut butter sandwiches does a student need to eat each week to consume the number of jars per year from part (b)?

20. Multiple Choice Belissa is now 18 years old. An 18-ounce jar of Belissa's favorite peanut butter costs $2.29. She reasons that her mom has spent about $2,300 on peanut butter for her since she was 5 years old. Which best describes her estimate?

   F. Less than the actual amount because she rounded the cost for a jar of peanut butter to the nearest dollar.

   G. Less than the actual amount because she rounded the cost of a jar of peanut butter to the nearest tenth of a dollar.

   H. More than the actual amount because she rounded the cost of a jar of peanut butter to the nearest dollar.

   J. More than the actual amount because she rounded the cost of a jar of peanut butter to the nearest tenth of a dollar.

21. a. A geyser is a spring from which columns of boiling water and steam erupt. Using the graph, describe the overall relationship between the height of an eruption and the time since the previous eruption.

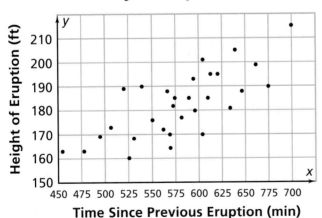

   b. The data above were collected for one particular geyser. What additional information would you need to decide whether the relationship in part (a) is true for most geysers?

This plot shows the number of hours students at a middle school spent doing homework one Monday. Use the plot for Exercises 22–24.

```
                Minutes Spent on Homework

                   Grade 6           Grade 8
             0 0 0 0 0 0 | 0 | 0
               5 5 5 5 5 5 | 1 | 0 5 5
                     5 0 0 | 2 | 0 0 0 5 5 5 5
                     5 5 5 | 3 | 0 0 0 0 5 5 5
                     5 5 0 | 4 | 0 0 0 5 5 5
                       0 0 | 5 | 0 5
    Key: 5 | 3 | 0 means 35   | 6 | 0 5 5
         minutes for Grade 6  0 | 7 | 5
         and 30 minutes for   5 | 8 | 0
         Grade 8
```

22. Find the median homework time for each grade.

23. **a.** For each grade, describe the variability in the distribution of homework times.

    b. Use statistics to explain how the times for sixth-graders compare to the times for eighth-graders.

24. Could these data be used to describe what is typical of all school nights in each of the two grades? Explain.

25. Consider the following data set: 20, 22, 23, 23, 24, 24, and 25.

    a. Find the mean and the range of the values.

    b. Add three values to the data set so that the mean of the new data set is greater than the mean of the original data set. What is the range of the new data set?

    c. Add three values to the original data set so that the mean of the new data set is less than the mean of the original data set. What is the range of the new data set?

    d. How do the ranges of the three data sets compare? Why do you think this is so?

26. Multiple Choice You survey 30 students from a population of 150 eighth-graders. Which statement is *not* correct?

   F. The ratio of those sampled to those not sampled is 30 to 120.

   G. One out of every five people in the population was sampled.

   H. Twenty-five percent of the students in the population were sampled.

   K. One fifth of the students in the population were sampled.

27. There are 350 students in a school. Ms. Cabral's class surveys two random samples of students to find out how many went to camp last summer. Here are the results:

       Sample 1: 8 of 25 attended camp

       Sample 2: 7 of 28 attended camp

   a. Based on the results from Sample 1, what fraction of the students in the school would you predict attended camp? How many students is this?

   b. Based on the results from Sample 2, what fraction of the students in the school would you predict attended camp? How many students is this?

   c. Which sample predicts that the greater fraction of students attended camp?

   d. One of Ms. Cabral's students says, "We were careful to choose our samples randomly. Why did the two samples give us different predictions?" How would you answer the student's question?

Annie's teacher starts each class with the names of all his students in a container. He chooses students to present answers by pulling out names at random. Once a name is chosen, it is set aside. There are 12 girls and 6 boys in the class.

28. What is the probability Annie will be the first student chosen on Monday?

29. What is the probability Annie will be the first student chosen on Tuesday?

30. What is the probability Annie will be the first student chosen on both Monday and Tuesday?

31. What is the probability the first student chosen on a given day will be a girl?

32. Suppose Annie is chosen first. What is the probability that the next student selected will be another girl?

33. Suppose the teacher plans to choose six students during one class. Would you be surprised if only two girls were chosen? Explain.

Go Online
PHSchool.com

For: Multiple-Choice Skills Practice
Web Code: apa-8254

Alyssa wants to know what students think about replacing the candy in two vending machines in the cafeteria with more healthful snacks. There are 300 sixth-graders, 300 seventh-graders, and 200 eighth-graders. Half of the students in each grade are girls. Alyssa obtains a list of student names, grouped by grade, with the girls listed first in each grade. Use this information for Exercises 34 and 35.

34. Alyssa randomly chooses 3 *different* students from the list of 800 students.

   a. What are the chances the first choice is a girl? The second choice is a girl? The third choice is a girl?

   b. What are the chances that Alyssa chooses three girls?

35. Alyssa decides to choose one person *from each grade* at random.

    a. What are the chances that her sixth-grade choice is a girl?

    b. What are the chances that she chooses three girls?

Alyssa chooses one girl and one boy from each grade. She asks each, "Which would you prefer, a machine with healthful snacks or a machine with candy?" Base your answers to Exercises 36–39 on her results below.

Vending Machine Survey Results

	Grade 6	Grade 7	Grade 8
Girl	healthful snack	healthful snack	healthful snack
Boy	candy	candy	healthful snack

36. Predict how many sixth-grade students prefer a machine with healthful snacks.

37. Predict how many students in the whole school prefer a machine with healthful snacks.

38. What is the probability that a student chosen at random from the whole school is an eighth-grader who prefers machine with healthful snacks?

39. What advice would you give Alyssa's principal about Alyssa's data and the two vending machines? Explain.

40. Alyssa's principal polls all 800 students and finds that 600 prefer a machine with healthful snacks.

    a. What is the probability that a randomly selected student prefers a machine with healthful snacks?

    b. What is the probability that a randomly selected student is a girl who prefers a machine with healthful snacks?

    c. What is the probability that a randomly selected student is a boy who prefers a machine with healthful snacks?

    d. What advice would you give the principal about the data collected and the vending machines?

Extensions

41. Television stations, radio stations, and newspapers often use polls to predict the winners of elections long before the votes are cast. What factors might cause a pre-election poll to be inaccurate?

42. Political parties often conduct their own pre-election polls to find out what voters think about their campaign and their candidates. How might a political party bias such a poll?

43. Find out how a local television station, radio station, or newspaper takes pre-election polls. Do you think the method they use is sensible?

44. a. Polls conducted prior to presidential elections commonly use samples of about 1,000 eligible voters. There are at most 203 million eligible voters in the United States. About what percent of eligible voters are in a sample of 1,000?

   b. How do you think this small sample is chosen so that the results will predict the winner with reasonable accuracy?

45. Use the table on the next page for parts (a)–(f).

   a. Pick your favorite jellybean color. From the table, select random samples of 5, 10, and 30 bags.

   b. For each bag in a sample, calculate the percent of your favorite color.

   c. For each sample size, make a line plot to display the distribution of the percent of your favorite color.

   d. Estimate the percent of your favorite color in all 100 bags.

   e. Predict the jellybean manufacturer's fixed percent of each color. Explain your reasoning.

Data From 100 Bags of Jellybeans

Bag	Green	Yellow	Orange	Blue	Brown	Red	Total
1	3	10	9	5	10	18	55
2	5	12	4	6	19	11	57
3	7	10	9	4	16	12	58
4	4	14	2	1	14	19	56
5	12	7	8	7	14	13	61
6	10	9	6	5	15	8	55
7	11	11	6	6	12	12	58
8	8	15	5	3	16	10	57
9	2	11	4	4	24	12	57
10	5	7	4	1	26	13	56
11	6	13	4	4	15	18	60
12	5	8	4	2	23	16	58
13	9	13	4	4	14	11	55
14	9	10	5	5	14	14	57
15	5	19	5	2	13	14	58
16	3	15	5	2	19	11	55
17	3	10	4	3	23	14	57
18	6	7	5	5	15	22	60
19	5	7	3	4	21	14	54
20	8	7	8	2	20	16	61
21	10	11	7	7	8	14	57
22	7	10	3	5	20	12	57
23	3	8	6	3	25	10	55
24	6	11	9	3	10	17	56
25	10	12	1	2	15	17	57
26	4	12	4	7	14	16	57
27	6	9	6	7	15	13	56
28	5	11	6	7	17	7	53
29	1	10	6	5	22	14	58
30	10	4	8	0	26	9	57
31	4	14	6	4	18	12	58
32	6	18	2	4	19	14	58
33	6	7	8	4	20	11	56
34	12	11	6	4	11	11	55
35	5	10	6	2	12	16	51
36	8	9	4	4	16	17	58
37	2	12	2	6	11	21	54
38	5	7	3	4	21	19	59
39	8	7	8	2	20	16	61
40	10	11	7	7	8	14	57
41	7	10	3	5	20	12	57
42	3	8	6	3	23	10	50
43	6	11	9	3	10	17	56
44	10	12	1	2	15	17	57
45	5	13	2	4	22	11	57
46	6	10	9	5	14	13	57
47	6	16	7	3	16	9	57
48	6	10	4	5	23	10	58
49	10	7	2	6	19	9	53
50	4	12	8	6	10	15	55

Bag	Green	Yellow	Orange	Blue	Brown	Red	Total
51	9	9	6	6	17	10	57
52	4	13	4	6	17	13	57
53	6	12	3	8	13	12	54
54	11	8	8	12	9	8	56
55	1	16	7	3	22	10	59
56	6	11	6	4	19	11	57
57	7	7	7	3	10	21	55
58	7	2	8	10	15	13	55
59	6	10	6	7	12	15	56
60	6	16	7	3	16	9	57
61	6	10	4	5	23	10	58
62	10	7	2	6	19	9	53
63	4	12	8	6	10	15	55
64	9	12	8	6	8	15	58
65	10	6	5	4	12	16	53
66	4	11	3	2	21	15	56
67	6	15	4	8	10	10	53
68	6	8	7	1	19	14	55
69	6	8	8	6	10	16	54
70	9	11	7	4	15	10	56
71	6	9	8	2	19	14	58
72	3	10	9	5	10	18	55
73	5	12	4	6	19	11	57
74	7	10	9	4	16	12	58
75	4	14	2	1	16	19	56
76	1	8	10	1	22	14	56
77	5	15	4	9	11	11	57
78	3	11	6	3	24	10	57
79	10	9	4	1	23	10	57
80	5	10	7	1	21	13	57
81	6	14	7	7	14	5	53
82	9	11	2	6	13	16	57
83	7	7	9	0	13	20	56
84	8	10	4	5	13	10	50
85	4	11	2	1	24	15	57
86	4	12	6	3	21	12	58
87	5	8	7	4	20	13	57
88	7	11	7	7	13	10	55
89	9	11	4	2	12	18	56
90	4	15	8	4	16	10	57
91	7	11	6	4	18	11	58
92	5	8	8	3	20	12	56
93	7	3	2	6	26	11	55
94	9	6	3	1	28	12	59
95	12	11	9	2	18	5	58
96	9	11	3	3	17	12	55
97	5	12	6	5	17	13	58
98	4	11	9	3	21	10	58
99	11	12	5	3	17	9	57
100	6	16	6	6	16	4	54

Mathematical Reflections 2

In this investigation, you learned about sampling techniques. You also made predictions about a population by examining data from random samples. The following questions will help you summarize what you have learned.

Think about your answers to these questions. Discuss your ideas with other students and your teacher. Then write a summary of your findings in your notebook.

1. Why are data often collected from a sample rather than from an entire population?

2. Describe several methods for selecting a sample from a population. Discuss the advantages and disadvantages of each method.

3. **a.** How are random samples different from convenience, self-selected, and systematic samples?

   b. Why is random sampling preferable to convenience, self-selected, or systematic sampling?

4. Describe three methods for selecting a random sample from a given population. What are the advantages and disadvantages of each method?

5. Suppose several random samples were selected from the same population. What similarities and differences would you expect to find in the medians, means, and ranges of the samples?

Investigation 3

Solving Real-World Problems

In this investigation, you will apply what you have learned about statistics to solve two real-world problems.

3.1 Solving an Archeological Mystery

Archeologists study past civilizations by excavating ancient settlements and examining the artifacts of the people who lived there.

On digs in southeastern Montana and north-central Wyoming, archeologists discovered the remains of two Native American settlements. They unearthed a number of arrowheads at both sites.

The tables below give the length, width, and neck width for each arrowhead the archeologists found. All measurements are in millimeters.

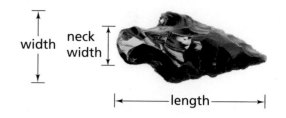

The archeologists hoped to use the arrowhead data to estimate the time period during which each site was inhabited.

Site I: 15 Arrowheads

Length (mm)	Width (mm)	Neck Width (mm)
24	19	8
27	19	10
29	19	11
29	22	12
31	16	12
31	32	16
37	23	11
38	22	12
38	26	14
40	25	16
45	22	11
45	28	15
55	22	13
62	26	14
63	29	18

SOURCE: *Plains Anthropologist*

Site II: 37 Arrowheads

Length (mm)	Width (mm)	Neck Width (mm)	Length (mm)	Width (mm)	Neck Width (mm)
13	10	6	24	13	8
15	11	7	24	13	8
16	12	8	24	14	10
16	13	7	24	15	9
17	15	9	24	15	8
18	12	10	25	13	7
19	12	8	25	13	7
19	13	9	25	15	10
20	12	7	25	24	7
20	12	9	26	14	10
21	11	7	26	14	11
22	13	9	26	15	11
22	13	9	27	14	8
22	13	8	28	11	6
22	14	10	28	13	9
23	14	9	32	12	8
23	15	9	42	16	11
24	11	8	43	14	9
24	12	7			

To help them with their work, the archeologists used arrowhead data from four other settlement sites. These data are given on the next page.

The archeologists knew the following:

- The Big Goose Creek and Wortham Shelter sites were settled between A.D. 500 and 1600.

- The Laddie Creek/Dead Indian Creek and Kobold/Buffalo Creek sites were settled between 4000 B.C. and A.D. 500.

How could you use these data to help you estimate the settlement periods for the new sites?

Big Goose Creek: 52 Arrowheads

Length (mm)	Width (mm)	Neck Width (mm)
16	13	9
16	14	10
17	13	8
17	13	10
18	12	7
18	12	8
18	13	7
18	13	8
18	15	11
19	11	8
20	11	6
20	12	8
21	11	7
21	12	7
21	12	9
22	12	9
22	13	8
22	13	10
23	13	8
23	13	9
23	14	9
24	14	9
24	14	11
25	13	7
25	13	8
25	14	8
26	11	8
26	12	12
26	14	9
26	16	10
27	13	9
27	13	9
27	14	9
27	14	9
27	17	13
28	10	5
28	13	7
28	15	9
29	15	8
30	11	7
30	13	8
30	14	8
30	14	8
30	14	9
30	15	11
31	12	8
33	13	7
33	15	9
34	15	9
35	14	10
39	18	12
40	14	8

Wortham Shelter: 45 Arrowheads

Length (mm)	Width (mm)	Neck Width (mm)
18	11	8
19	12	9
19	14	10
19	14	10
19	16	14
20	13	8
20	14	10
20	15	11
22	12	9
22	14	8
23	13	11
23	14	11
23	15	11
24	12	9
24	13	10
25	14	8
25	14	10
25	15	10
25	15	10
25	15	12
26	13	9
26	13	10
26	15	12
27	14	8
27	14	10
27	15	11
28	13	11
28	14	10
28	16	12
29	13	10
29	14	9
29	14	9
29	17	12
30	14	11
30	16	9
30	17	14
31	13	10
31	14	10
31	14	11
31	16	12
31	17	12
32	14	7
32	15	10
35	18	14
42	18	7

Laddie Creek/ Dead Indian Creek: 18 Arrowheads

Length (mm)	Width (mm)	Neck Width (mm)
25	18	13
27	20	13
27	20	14
29	14	11
29	20	13
30	23	13
31	18	11
32	16	10
32	19	10
35	20	15
37	17	13
38	17	14
39	18	15
40	18	11
41	15	11
42	22	12
44	18	13
52	21	16

Kobold/ Buffalo Creek: 52 Arrowheads

Length (mm)	Width (mm)	Neck Width (mm)
25	18	15
30	17	12
30	19	15
31	16	13
31	17	12
32	20	13
32	22	17
32	23	18
35	19	11
35	22	14
37	18	12
37	21	11
38	18	9
38	24	15
39	21	14
40	19	15
40	20	12
40	20	13
40	21	12
41	21	13
42	22	14
42	22	15
44	20	11
44	20	12
44	25	14
45	20	13
45	22	13
46	17	13
46	20	14
46	23	14
47	19	13
47	20	12
47	22	13
49	20	14
50	21	13
50	23	15
50	23	16
51	18	10
52	17	12
52	22	15
52	24	16
54	24	13
56	19	12
56	21	15
56	25	13
57	22	15
61	19	12
64	21	13
66	20	15
67	21	13
71	24	13
80	25	11

SOURCE: *Plains Anthropologist*

Problem 3.1 Comparing and Analyzing Data

The archeologists hypothesized that Native Americans inhabiting the same area of the country during the same time period would have fashioned similar tools.

A. Use box plots to compare the lengths of the arrowheads discovered at the new sites with the lengths of those from the known sites.

   1. Based on your comparisons, during which time period (4000 B.C. to A.D. 500, or A.D. 500 to 1600) do you think Site I was settled? Explain how your statistics and graphs support your answers.

   2. During which time period do you think Site II was settled? Explain how your statistics and graphs support your answers.

B. Use box plots to compare the widths of the arrowheads discovered at the new sites with the widths of those from the known sites. Do your findings support your answers from Question A? Explain.

C. Suppose the archeologists had collected only a few arrowheads from each new site. Might they have reached a different conclusion? Explain.

ACE **Homework starts on page 54.**

3.2 Simulating Cookies

Jeff and Ted operate the Custom Cookie Counter. Their advertising slogan is "Five giant chocolate chips in every cookie!"

One day, a customer complains when she finds only three chocolate chips in her cookie. Jeff thinks she must have miscounted because he mixes 60 chips into every batch of a dozen cookies.

Jeff and Ted examine a batch of cookies fresh from the oven. The drawing on the right shows what they find.

Getting Ready for Problem **3.2**

- What is wrong with Jeff's reasoning about how many chocolate chips to add to each batch of cookie dough?

- What advice would you give to Jeff and Ted to help them solve their quality-control problem?

Ted wants to figure out how many chocolate chips they should add to each batch of dough to be fairly confident each cookie will have five chips. He comes up with an idea that involves random sampling. He explains his idea to Jeff.

"Think of a batch of dough as 12 cookies packed in a bowl. As we add chips to the dough, each chip lands in one of the cookies. There is an equally likely chance that a chip will land in any 1 of the 12 cookies."

"We can simulate adding the chips by generating random integers from 1 to 12. A 1 means a chip is added to cookie 1, a 2 means a chip is added to cookie 2, and so on.

"We can keep a tally of where the 'chips' land and stop when each 'cookie' contains at least five chips. The total number will be an estimate of the number of chips we need to add to each batch."

Jeff says, "If we only do this once, we might need only 60 chips. If we do it again, we might need 90. Some cookies might be loaded with chips before every cookie gets five chips. We need to repeat the experiment enough times to find a typical result."

A. 1. Conduct the simulation Ted describes. Use a chart like the one at the right.

2. Find the total number of chips in the entire batch.

B. 1. Make a histogram of the total number of chips from each student in your class.

2. Describe what your histogram shows about the distribution of the results.

3. Make a box plot of the total number of chips from each student in your class.

4. Describe what your box plot shows about the distribution of the results.

Cookie Number	Number of Chips per Cookie
1	
2	
3	
4	
5	
6	
7	
8	
9	
10	
11	
12	

C. Jeff and Ted want to be sure that most of the time there will be at least five chips in each cookie. However, they don't want to waste money by mixing in too many chips. Based on your class data and the two representations you made, how many chips would you advise them to use in each batch? Explain.

D. 1. As a class, discuss students' recommendations from Question C. Choose a number the whole class can agree on.

2. Conduct 30 simulations to randomly distribute the recommended number of chips among the 12 cookies. For each simulation, record whether each cookie has at least five chips. Organize your information in a table like the one at the right.

Simulation Trial Number	Did Each Cookie Have at Least Five Chips?
1	
2	
3	
4	
⋮	
30	

3. What percent of the time did your simulation give at least five chips per cookie?

4. Using the distribution of your simulation results, make a final recommendation to Jeff and Ted about how many chips to put in each batch. Justify your choice.

5. Suggest what Jeff and Ted might say to promote their cookies in a more accurate way.

ACE **Homework starts on page 54.**

Applications

1. a. Refer to the arrowhead tables from Problem 3.1. These data include the neck width of each arrowhead. Calculate the five-number summaries of the neck-width data for all six sites (the two new sites and the four known sites).

neck width

    b. On the same scale, make a box plot of the neck-width data for each site.

    c. Based on your results from parts (a) and (b), during which time periods do you think Sites I and II were settled? Explain.

2. a. A baker makes raisin muffins in batches of four dozen. She pours a box of raisins into each batch. How could you use a sample from a batch of muffins to estimate the number of raisins in a box?

    b. There are 1,000 raisins in a box. How many raisins would you expect to find in a typical muffin? Explain.

3. Keisha opens a bag containing 60 chocolate chip cookies. She selects a sample of 20 cookies and counts the chips in each one. She records her data in the table shown.

Estimate the number of chocolate chips in the bag. Explain.

Cookie	Chips		Cookie	Chips
1	6		11	8
2	8		12	7
3	8		13	9
4	11		14	9
5	7		15	8
6	6		16	6
7	6		17	8
8	7		18	10
9	11		19	10
10	7		20	8

4. Use Keisha's data from Exercise 3. Copy and complete each statement with the most appropriate fraction: $\frac{1}{4}$, $\frac{1}{6}$, or $\frac{1}{2}$.

More than __?__ of the cookies have at least 8 chips.

More than __?__ of the cookies have at least 9 chips.

More than __?__ of the cookies have at least 10 chips.

5. Yung-nan wants to estimate the number of beans in a large jar. She takes out 150 beans, marks each with a red dot, returns them to the jar, and mixes them with the unmarked beans. She then takes four samples from the jar.

Bean Samples

Sample	Total Beans	Beans With Red Dots
1	25	3
2	150	23
3	75	15
4	250	25

a. Which sample has the greatest percent of beans that are marked with red dots? Use this sample to predict the number of beans in the jar.

b. The shaded bars below are a visual way to think about making a prediction from Sample 3. Explain what the bars show and how they can be used to estimate the number of beans in the whole jar.

Sample 3
Beans in sample: 75

15, or 20% marked				

Whole Jar
Beans in entire jar: ?

150, or 20% marked				

c. Which sample has the least percent of beans that are marked with red dots? Use this sample to predict the number of beans in the jar.

d. What is your best guess for the total number of beans in the jar?

6. After testing many samples, an electric company determines that approximately 2 of every 1,000 light bulbs on the market are defective. Suppose Americans buy over a billion light bulbs every year. Estimate how many of these bulbs are defective.

7. **Multiple Choice** After testing many samples, a milk shipper determines that approximately 3 in every 100 cartons of milk leak. The company ships 200,000 cartons of milk every week. About how many of these cartons leak?

   A. 3   **B.** 600   **C.** 2,000   **D.** 6,000

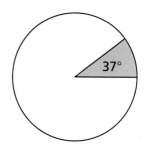
Go Online
PHSchool.com
For: Multiple-Choice Skills Practice
Web Code: apa-8354

Connections

8. **Multiple Choice** The circle graph shows data for 1,585 students. Which is the best approximation of the number of students represented by the pink sector?

   F. 40   **G.** 160   **H.** 590   **J.** 58,650

37°

To monitor driving speeds, states set up radar checkpoints to measure the speeds of samples of drivers. Use this information for Exercises 9 and 10.

9. Suppose you want to show that drivers in your state generally obey speed limits. Where and when would you set up radar checkpoints?

10. Suppose you want to show that drivers in your state often exceed speed limits. Where and when would you set up radar checkpoints?

11. Sometimes graphs can be misleading. The graphs below all display the same data about the percent of newspapers recycled from 1993 to 2004.

Homework Help nline PHSchool.com

For: Help with Exercise 11
Web Code: ape-8311

a. Which graph do you think gives the clearest picture of the data pattern? Why?

b. Why are the other graphs misleading?

Number of Recycled Newspapers 1993–2004

Graph W

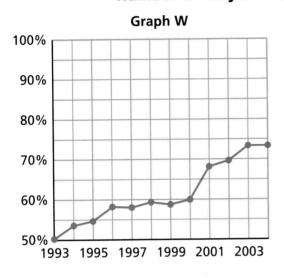

Graph X

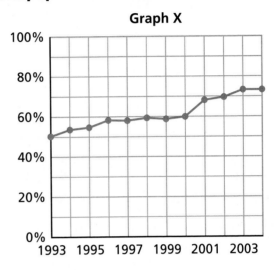

Graph Y

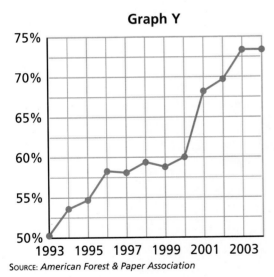

Graph Z

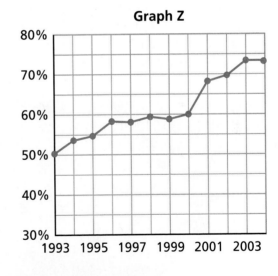

Source: *American Forest & Paper Association*

For Exercises 12–16, use these and other questions to analyze each survey.

- What is the goal of the survey?
- What is the population being studied?
- How is the sample chosen?
- How is the data analyzed and reported?
- Does the analysis support the conclusions?

12. In designing a remote control, representatives for a television manufacturer call 1,000 households with television sets. They find that remote-control users sit an average of 3 meters from their television sets. Based on this finding, the manufacturer designs the remote control to work well at distances of 2.5 meters to 3.5 meters from a television set.

13. A lightbulb manufacturer wants to know the "defect rate" for its product. One morning, the manager takes 10 boxes of 50 lightbulbs from the assembly line and tests them. All but five bulbs work. The manager concludes that production quality is acceptable.

14. A nutritionist wants to know what percent of Calories in a typical United States teenager's diet are from fat. She asks health teachers in Dallas, Texas, to have their students keep logs of what they eat on one school day. The nutritionist analyzes the logs and finds that the median intake was 500 fat Calories per day, which is the recommended daily allowance. She concludes that Calories from fat are not a problem in the diets of teenagers.

15. A cookie maker claims that there are over 1,000 chocolate chips in a bag of its cookies. A skeptical consumer calls the company and asks how they know this. A spokesperson says they chose a sample of bags of cookies, soaked each bag in cold water to remove all the dough, and weighed the chips that remained. In each case, the chips weighed more than a bag of 1,000 chocolate chips.

16. In the cafeteria line, Sam wrinkles his nose when he sees salami subs. When the cook asks what he would prefer, Sam replies, "I like bologna better." The cook surveys the next ten students. Seven students say they prefer bologna to salami. The cook decides to serve bologna subs instead of salami subs in the future.

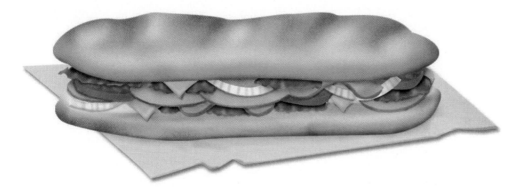

For Exercises 17–21, use the box plot below. Tell whether each statement is true. Explain.

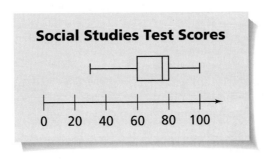

17. The class median is less than 80.

18. Half the class scored between 60 and 80.

19. At least one student earned a score of 100.

20. The class mean is probably less than the median.

21. If there are 30 students in the class, at least 10 scored above 80.

Extensions

22. A company produces pushpins in the percents shown in the table. The school secretary opens a large bag of pushpins. She puts the pins into small boxes to distribute to teachers. She puts 50 pins in each box.

Percent of Pushpins of Each Color

Color	Percent
white	15%
yellow	10%
red	15%
orange	20%
green	15%
blue	25%

a. How many pushpins of each color do you expect to be in a box?

b. How do you expect the number of pushpins of each color to vary across the samples?

c. You can simulate filling the boxes by generating random integers from 1 to 20. Which numbers would you let represent each color? How many random numbers do you need to generate to simulate filling one box?

d. Carry out the simulation described in part (c) three times. Compare the distributions of colors in your simulated samples with the expected distribution from part (a).

e. Suppose the secretary selects a random sample of 1,000 pushpins from the bag. How closely would you expect the percent of each color in her sample to match the percent in the table?

23. You can use a simulation to help you answer this question:

If you select five students at random from your class, what is the probability that at least two will have the same birth month?

a. Design a simulation to model this situation. Tell which month each simulation outcome represents.

b. Use your birth-month simulation to produce at least 25 samples of five people. Use your results to estimate the probability that at least two people in a group of five will have the same birth month.

c. Explain how you could revise your simulation to explore this question:

What are the chances that at least two students in a class of 25 have the same birthday (month and day, but not year)?

Mathematical Reflections 3

In this investigation, you applied your knowledge of statistics and data displays to solve real-world problems. These questions will help you summarize what you have learned.

Think about your answers to these questions. Discuss your ideas with other students and your teacher. Then write a summary of your findings in your notebook.

1. How can you use statistics to
   a. compare samples?
   b. draw conclusions about the population from which each sample was selected?

2. In what ways can you expect the distribution of data values for a sample to be similar to and different from the distribution of data values for the entire population from which samples were selected?

Relating Two Variables

Box plots and histograms allow you to look at one variable at a time. For example, you can use box plots to study the quality ratings of peanut butters. What if you wanted to study how the price of a peanut butter is related to its quality rating?

Finding the answer requires looking at how two variables are related. A **scatter plot** allows you to look at two variables at once. The scatter plot at the right shows (*quality rating, price*) pairs for each of the 37 types of peanut butter you studied in Investigation 1.

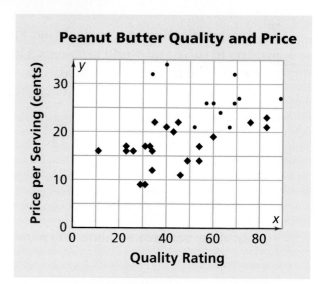

Peanut Butter Quality and Price

4.1 Are Quality Ratings and Prices Related?

Each point on the scatter plot gives you two pieces of information. For example, the point (60, 26) represents a peanut butter with a quality rating of 60 and a price of $0.26 per serving.

Problem 4.1 Interpreting Scatter Plots

A. Which symbol on the scatter plot represents data for the natural peanut butters? Which symbol is for the regular peanut butters?

B. What appears to be true about the prices of peanut butters with high quality ratings? With low quality ratings? Is there a relationship between quality rating and price? Explain.

C. Do any (*quality rating, price*) pairs appear to be unusual? Explain.

D. 1. How can you use the scatter plot to compare the quality ratings of natural with regular peanut butters?

   2. How can you use the scatter plot to compare the prices of natural with regular peanut butters?

ACE Homework starts on page 69.

Writing an Equation to Describe a Relationship

In *Data About Us*, a group of 54 sixth-grade students measured their arm spans and their heights. Their data are shown in the scatter plot.

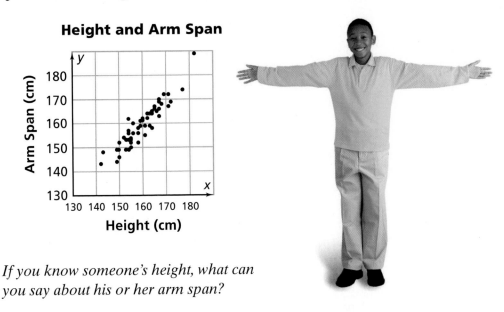

Height and Arm Span

If you know someone's height, what can you say about his or her arm span?

Getting Ready for Problem

Find a line to model the trend in the data.

• Where does your line cross the *y*-axis?

• What is the *y*-coordinate of the point on the line with an *x*-coordinate of 190?

• What is the *x*-coordinate of the point with a *y*-coordinate of 175?

Problem 4.2 Writing an Equation to Describe a Relationship

A. Consider a line through (130, 130) and (190, 190).

1. How might you use this line to describe the relationship between height and arm span?

2. Write an equation for this line using *h* for height and *a* for arm span.

3. What is true about the relationship between height and arm span for the points on the line? For the points above the line? For the points below the line?

Investigation 4 Relating Two Variables **63**

B. 1. Make a scatter plot of the (*body length, wingspan*) data from the table.

Airplane Comparisons

Plane	Engine Type	Body Length (m)	Wingspan (m)
Boeing 707	jet	46.6	44.4
Boeing 747	jet	70.7	59.6
Ilyushin IL-86	jet	59.5	48.1
McDonnell Douglas DC-8	jet	57.1	45.2
Antonov An-124	jet	69.1	73.3
British Aerospace 146	jet	28.6	26.3
Lockheed C-5 Galaxy	jet	75.5	67.9
Antonov An-225	jet	84.0	88.4
Airbus A300	jet	54.1	44.9
Airbus A310	jet	46.0	43.9
Airbus A320	jet	37.5	33.9
Boeing 737	jet	33.4	28.9
Boeing 757	jet	47.3	38.1
Boeing 767	jet	48.5	47.6
Lockheed Tristar L-1011	jet	54.2	47.3
McDonnell Douglas DC-10	jet	55.5	50.4
Aero/Boeing Spacelines Guppy	propeller	43.8	47.6
Douglas DC-4 C-54 Skymaster	propeller	28.6	35.8
Douglas DC-6	propeller	32.2	35.8
Lockheed L-188 Electra	propeller	31.8	30.2
Vickers Viscount	propeller	26.1	28.6
Antonov An-12	propeller	33.1	38.0
de Havilland DHC Dash-7	propeller	24.5	28.4
Lockheed C-130 Hercules/L-100	propeller	34.4	40.4
British Aerospace 748/ATP	propeller	26.0	30.6
Convair 240	propeller	24.1	32.1
Curtiss C-46 Commando	propeller	23.3	32.9
Douglas DC-3	propeller	19.7	29.0
Grumman Gulfstream I/I-C	propeller	19.4	23.9
Ilyushin IL-14	propeller	22.3	31.7
Martin 4-0-4	propeller	22.8	28.4
Saab 340	propeller	19.7	21.4

SOURCE: *Airport Airplanes*

2. Does your equation relating height and arm span from Question A also describe the relationship between body length and wingspan for airplanes? Explain.

3. Predict the wingspan of an airplane with a body length of 40 meters.

4. Predict the body length of an airplane with a wingspan of 60 meters.

C. 1. Use the scatter plot below. Does your equation relating height and arm span from Question A also describe the relationship between body length and wingspan for birds? Explain.

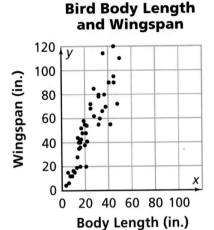

Bird Body Length and Wingspan

2. Find a line that fits the overall pattern of points. What is the equation of your line?

3. Predict the wingspan for a bird whose body length is 60 inches. Explain.

ACE Homework starts on page 69.

4.3 Human Development Index and Life Expectancies

The Human Development Index (HDI) is a number used to report how well a country is doing in overall human development. The HDI measures the average achievement in three basic dimensions of human development—a long and healthy life, access to education, and a decent standard of living.

Countries with an HDI of over 0.800 are part of the high human development group. Countries from 0.500 to 0.800 are part of the medium group. Countries below 0.500 are part of the low group.

Problem 4.3 Analyzing a Relationship

A. 1. Describe the variability in the data in the histogram.

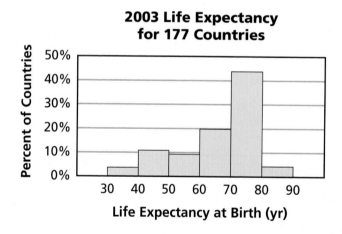

2003 Life Expectancy for 177 Countries

2. Estimate the percent of the countries with life expectancies of 60 years or greater.

3. Use the box plots. Describe how the life expectancies of the countries with upper and medium HDIs compare with the life expectancies of countries with low HDIs.

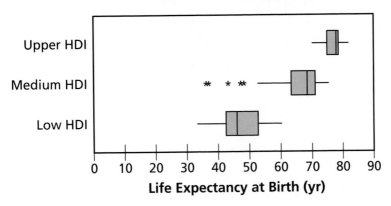

2003 Life Expectancy and HDI for 177 Countries

4. The medium HDI group has outliers. Using the table, identify which countries are the outliers. Explain.

2003 Life Expectancy and HDI

Country	Life Expectancy at Birth (yr)	HDI
Lao People's Dem. Rep.	54.7	0.545
Botswana	36.3	0.565
Zimbabwe	36.9	0.505
South Africa	48.4	0.658
Equatorial Guinea	43.3	0.655
India	63.3	0.602
Namibia	48.3	0.627
Uganda	47.3	0.508

SOURCE: *United Nations Development Programme*

B. Use a straightedge to locate the line $y = 0.01325x - 0.166$ on the scatter plot shown below. **Hint:** Use the equation to find two points, $(0, y_1)$ and $(80, y_2)$, on the line.

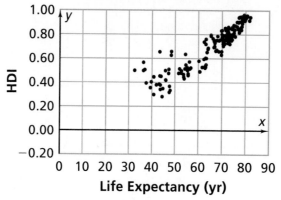

2003 Life Expectancy and HDI for 177 Countries

SOURCE: *United Nations Development Programme*

1. How well does this line model the relationship between life expectancy and HDI?

2. Use this line to estimate the HDI for $x = 90$ years.

3. Describe how you can use this line to estimate HDI when you know life expectancy.

ACE Homework starts on page 69.

Applications

1. a. Compare the values in the peanut butter comparison table in Problem 1.1 to the points on the scatter plot. Why are some points located on or very near the horizontal axis?

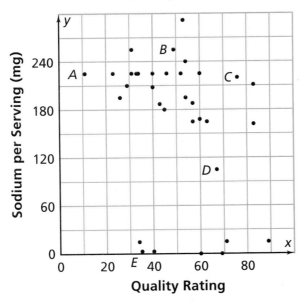

Peanut Butter Quality and Sodium Content

b. Give the approximate coordinates of each labeled point. Explain what the coordinates tell you about the peanut butter represented by the point.

c. Jeff says, "Most peanut butters, no matter what their quality rating, have between 160 and 240 milligrams of sodium per serving." Do you agree or disagree? Explain.

Nutrition Facts		
Serving Size 2 Tbsp (32g)		
Servings Per Container about 15		

Amount Per Serving		
Calories 190 Calories from Fat 140		

	% Daily Value*
Total Fat 17g	**26%**
Saturated Fat 3.5g	**18%**
Cholesterol 0 mg	**0%**
Sodium 150mg	**6%**

	% Daily Value*
Total Carbohydrate 7g	**2%**
Dietary Fiber 2g	**8%**
Sugars 3g	
Protein 7g	

Vitamin A 0% • Vitamin C 0%
Calcium 0% • Iron 2% Niacin
20% Vitamin E 10%

*Percent Daily Values are based on a 2,000 calorie diet.

2. a. Plot the (*height, arm span*) data from the table below.

Student Measurement Data

Gender	Height (cm)	Arm Span (cm)	Foot Length (cm)
F	160	158	25
M	111	113	15
F	160	160	23
F	152	155	23.5
F	146	144	24
F	157	156	24
M	136	135	21
F	143	142	23
M	147	145	20
M	133	133	20
F	153	151	25
M	148	149	23
M	125	123	20
F	150	149	20

b. Draw the line $y = x$ on your scatter plot.

c. Explain how this line can be used to describe the relationship between height and arm span.

d. Plot the (*height, foot length*) data.

e. Experiment with different lines to see if you can find one that fits the data. You might try $y = \frac{1}{2}x$ or $y = \frac{1}{3}y$. Give the equation of a line that "fits" the data.

3. This scatter plot shows (*length, width*) data for the arrowheads found at Kobold/Buffalo Creek (see Problem 3.1).

Kobold/Buffalo Creek Arrowheads

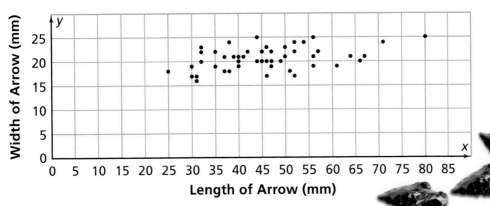

a. Estimate the range of the lengths.

b. Estimate the range of the widths.

c. Shannon drew the line $y = 20$. Do you think it gives a good estimate of the relationship between length and width? Explain.

d. Suppose you know the width of an arrowhead from the site that is not on the scatter plot. Can you predict its length? Explain.

For: Multiple-Choice Skills Practice
Web Code: apa-8454

Connections

For Exercises 4–6, use the graph below. There are two sections to the graph:

- The top section shows information about the world and about developing and least developed countries.

- The bottom section shows different continents.

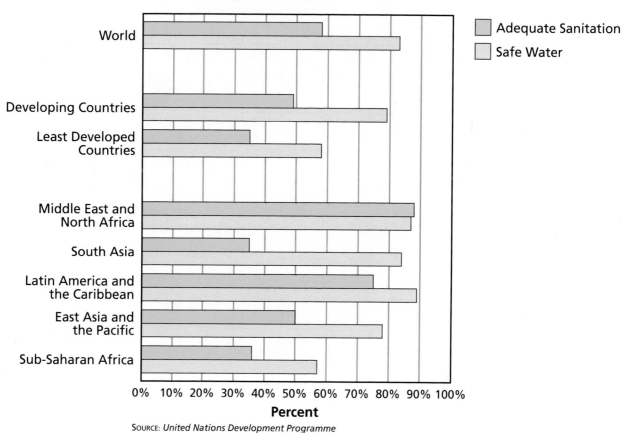

Access to Safe Water and Adequate Sanitation—2002

SOURCE: *United Nations Development Programme*

4. Write three comparison statements about the data.

5. Fill in the missing information to make a true statement.

   With the exception of _?_ and _?_, at least 50% of the population of each region has access to adequate sanitation.

6. **Multiple Choice** Tell which fraction completes this statement:

   In _?_ of the regions, less than 75% of the population has access to safe water.

   A. $\frac{1}{5}$ **B.** $\frac{2}{5}$ **C.** $\frac{3}{5}$ **D.** $\frac{4}{5}$

7. A different type of scatter plot is shown at the right. Some of the peanut butters have the same price per serving and sodium content. When this happens, the "dots" are placed on top of each other so they slightly overlap. Suppose you know the price per serving for a peanut butter. Can you predict the amount of sodium in a serving? Explain.

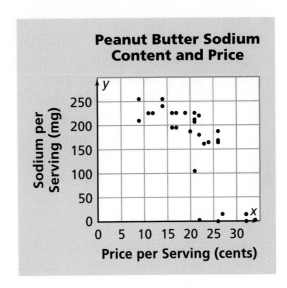

8. Using the data from the scatter plot in Exercise 7, tell which title matches each histogram below.

Title 1: Distribution of Price per Serving

Title 2: Distribution of Sodium per Serving

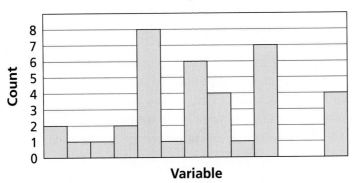

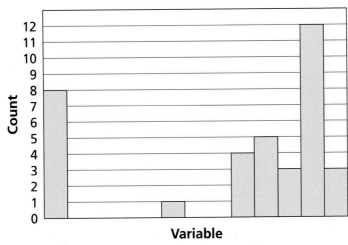

9. **a.** Refer to the Airplane Data from Problem 4.2. Make two histograms that allow you to compare the body lengths of propeller planes with those of jet planes. Experiment with interval widths of 5 or 10 meters. (Remember to use the same interval width on both graphs.)

b. Determine the mean, median, and range for the body lengths of the propeller planes.

c. Determine the mean, median, and range for the body lengths of the jet planes.

d. Write three statements comparing the body lengths of propeller airplanes with the body lengths of jet airplanes.

For Exercises 10–13, write an equation for the line through the pair of points.

10. $(2, 3)$ and $(1, 6)$

11. $(0, 2)$ and $(-2, 7)$

12. $(-1, 0)$ and $(-2, -6)$

13. $(3, 7)$ and $(1, 8)$

Multiple Choice Experts say that for every 20 pounds of body weight, you should carry only 3 pounds in a backpack. This means that your backpack should weigh no more than 15% of your body weight. Complete each sentence in Exercises 14–17 to make a true statement using the box plots on the facing page.

14. At least ■ of students in seventh grade carry backpacks that are heavier than 15% of their body weight.

   F. 25%   **G.** 50%   **H.** 75%   **J.** 100%

15. Over ■ of students in third grade carry backpacks that are in the acceptable weight range.

   A. 25%   **B.** 50%   **C.** 75%   **D.** 100%

16. Between ■ of boys carry backpacks that are in the acceptable range.

   F. 0 and 25%   **G.** 25% and 50%

   H. 50% and 75%   **J.** 75% and 100%

17. Between ■ of girls carry backpacks that are not in the acceptable range.

   A. 0 and 25%   **B.** 25% and 50%

   C. 50% and 75%   **D.** 75% and 100%

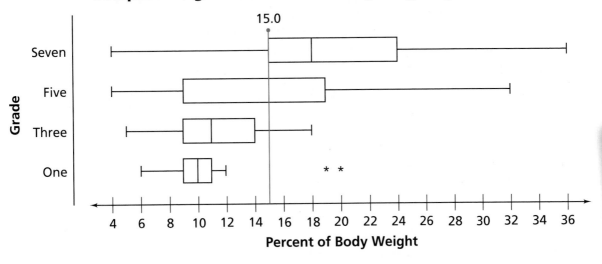

Backpack Weight as a Percent of Body Weight by Grade

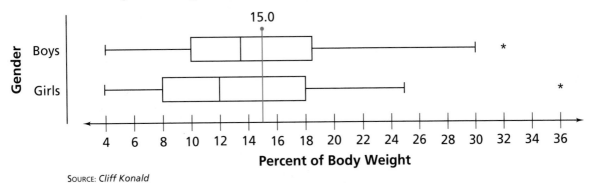

Backpack Weight as a Percent of Body Weight by Gender

SOURCE: *Cliff Konald*

Tell whether each statement is true or false using the box plots above. Explain your reasoning.

18. Students in grades five and seven carry more backpack weight compared to body weight than do students in first or third grades.

19. Girls carry at least twice as much backpack weight compared to body weight as boys do.

20. The data for students in grade one has the most outliers.

21. The school Sam attends sells backpacks as a fundraiser. The school needs to sell $3,600 to earn enough to have a dance. Grade 6 collected $736.25. Grade 7 collected $1,211.25. Grade 8 collected $1,591.25. Sam says they have raised enough for the dance. He rounded the three totals to $800, $1,200, and $1,600 to get exactly $3,600. Is his estimate a good one? Why or why not?

22. Multiple Choice Sam's school bought some new technology equipment. They spent $2,089.98 on graphing calculators, $398.75 on motion detectors for experiments, and $4,456.20 on computers. The school will pay the bill in 12 equal installments. What is a reasonable amount for each payment?

F. $100

G. $500

H. $600

J. $1,000

For Exercises 23–25, use the box plot to choose one of the following numbers to make a correct statement: 75, 99, 106, 127, 151. Give evidence from the box plot to support each answer.

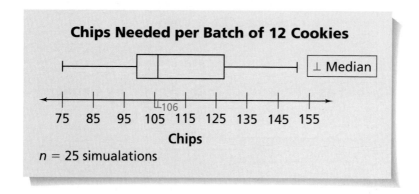

23. Half of all successful batches use fewer than __?__ chips.

24. You should add at least __?__ chips if you want to make a successful batch at least 75% of the time.

25. You should add at least __?__ chips if you want to make a successful batch at least 25% of the time.

26. Multiple Choice Which equation best fits the data in the graph?

A. $y = x$

B. $y = 7x$

C. $y = \frac{x}{7}$

D. There is too little information to know.

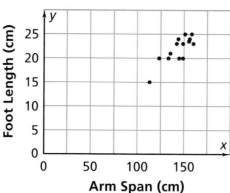

For a class project, students collect data about the number of boys or girls in the families of their classmates. Use the table below to answer Exercises 27–30.

Name	Number of Boys in the Family	Number of Girls in the Family
Anya	0	2
Brian	8	0
Charlie	1	2
Diane	0	1
Elisha	1	1
Felix	2	0
Gloria	0	2
Han	1	2
Ivan	1	1
Jorge	4	1

27. Anya wants to make a Venn diagram with the groups "Has Boys in the Family" and "Has Girls in the Family." She begins by placing herself on the diagram. Copy and complete her diagram below.

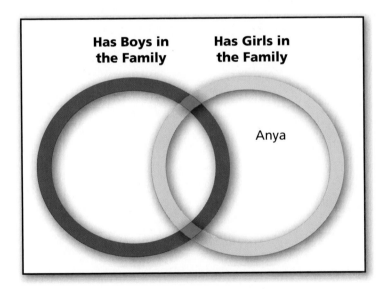

28. Make a bar graph that shows that the usual number of children in the family is two and that Brian's family is unusual.

29. Charlie wants to make a circle graph. What could the parts of the circle be labeled?

30. Make a graph to see if there is any relationship between the number of boys in a family and the number of girls in a family.

An Honor Society shovels snow for senior citizens on weekends. Some students can shovel only on Fridays, some can shovel only on Saturdays, some can shovel only on Sundays, some can shovel two out of three days, and some can shovel all three days. Justin is organizing this project and must report on it at the end of the school year.

For Exercises 31–35, decide which of these five representations Justin should choose. Explain why.

box plot   Venn diagram   circle graph
value bar graph   back-to-back stem-and-leaf plot

31. Justin wants to know whom he can call on any snowy weekend day.

32. At the end of a month, Justin wants to show how many hours each person shoveled snow.

33. The Honor Society worked on the same project last year. Justin wants to compare the hours members spent shoveling snow this year with the hours spent shoveling snow last year.

34. The Honor Society performs four other service projects in addition to shoveling snow. Justin wants to report how the total hours spent on all the projects was divided among the five projects.

35. Some members contribute a lot of time and other just a little. Justin wants to make a graph that shows what is a typical time commitment, what is an outstanding time commitment, and what is an unusually low time commitment. He does not want to show individual names.

Extensions

36. a. The graph below models the relationship between a pumpkin's circumference and its weight. Suppose that, instead of being modeled by this curve, the relationship was modeled by the line $y = x$. What would this indicate about how the weight of a pumpkin changes as the circumference increases?

Pumpkin Measurements

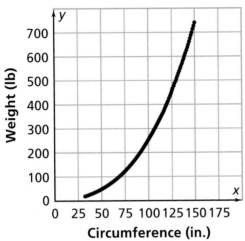

b. Describe what the actual curve indicates about how the weight of a pumpkin changes as the circumference increases.

Mathematical Reflections 4

In this investigation, you made scatter plots to look for relationships between pairs of variables. Where possible, you drew a line to fit the pattern in the points, and used the line to predict the value of one variable given the value of the other. These questions will help you summarize what you have learned.

Think about your answers to these questions. Discuss your ideas with other students and your teacher. Then write a summary of your findings in your notebook.

1. Describe some situations you explored in which the values of two variables are related in a predictable way. For example, you saw that you can estimate a person's arm span if you know his or her height.

2. Describe some situations you explored in which the values of two variables are not related in a predictable way. For example, as the lengths of the arrowheads increase, the widths do not increase in a regular pattern.

3. What does it mean to say one variable *is related to* another variable? Think about your answers to Questions 1 and 2.

Unit Project

Estimating a Deer Population

The statewide deer population in Michigan is estimated to be about 1.7 million.

How is it possible to estimate the deer population of a state, or even of a small part of a state?

The *capture-tag-recapture* method is one way of estimating a deer population. Biologists capture deer in a targeted area, tag them, and then release them. Later, they capture deer and count the number with tags to estimate the population of deer in the targeted area.

You can simulate the *capture-tag-recapture* method by using a container filled with white beans. Think of each bean as a deer in the upper peninsula of Michigan. Your job is to estimate the number of deer without actually counting them all.

Work with your group to perform the experiment described below.

Materials

a container with a lid

a package of white beans (about two cups)

a marker

Collect the Data

- Remove 100 beans from the container and mark them with a pen or marker.

- Put the marked beans back into the container and mix them with the unmarked beans.

- Without looking at the beans, one person should scoop out 25 beans from the jar. Record the number of marked and unmarked beans in this sample. Then, return the beans to the jar and mix the beans. Repeat this until everyone in your group has chosen a sample.

- Repeat the scoop-and-count procedure for samples of 50, 75, and 100 beans. For each sample, record the number of marked and unmarked beans.

Analyze and Summarize the Data

1. Find the percent of "deer" in each of your group's samples. Make one or more representations of these data.

2. Use tables, graphs, and statistics to analyze the data you collected.

3. Use your analysis to estimate the number of "deer" in your container.

4. Prepare a report about your experiment and findings. Be sure to include the following:

   - A discussion of how you investigated the problem

   - An analysis and summary of the data you collected, including tables, graphs, and statistics

   - An estimate of the number of "deer" in your container and an explanation of how you made this estimate

   You might also do Internet research on the following topics and include your findings in your report:

   - Other methods used to count deer

   - Methods used to count whales, salmon, prairie dogs, or other animals

Looking Back and Looking Ahead

Unit Review

In this unit, you collected, organized, and displayed sample data. You learned how to choose samples and how to compare samples in order to draw conclusions about the population from which they were taken. You also looked at the ways two attributes of a sample might be related.

Go Online
PHSchool.com

For: Vocabulary Review Puzzle
Web Code: apj-8051

Use Your Understanding: Statistical Reasoning

Test your understanding and skill in the use of samples to describe populations by solving these problems that arose during a nutrition discussion in a health class.

1. One student claims that stores promote sales of cereals with high sugar content by putting them on low shelves, where children can see them.

   To test this claim, the class collects data for 77 different cereals. For each cereal, they record the sugar content and calories per serving and whether the cereal is on the top, middle, or bottom shelf.

   These plots show the sugar content of the cereals on each shelf.

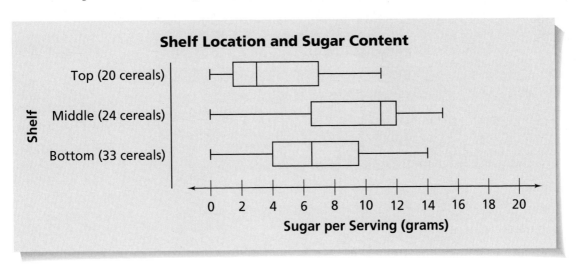

a. What is the range of sugar content for cereals on the top shelf? For cereals on the middle shelf? For cereals on the bottom shelf?

b. Estimate the median sugar content for the cereals on each shelf.

c. How many of the 20 top-shelf cereals have a sugar content greater than or equal to the upper quartile?

d. What percent of the 33 bottom-shelf cereals have a sugar content at least as great as the lower quartile but no greater than the upper quartile?

e. Does there seem to be a pattern relating sugar content and shelf placement for cereals?

f. The top shelf, middle shelf, and bottom shelf have different numbers of cereals. How does using a box plot make it easy to compare the three distributions?

g. Suppose you collected data from a sample of cereals in a supermarket near you. What do you think you would find out about the sugar content in cereals on different shelves?

2. Jerome wants to make a scatter plot to see if there is a relationship between sugar content and calories for the cereals. Instead of looking at data for all 77 cereals, he decides to choose a sample of 25. He considers three ways of selecting a sample.

● Method 1: List the 77 cereals in alphabetical order. Include every third cereal in the sample.

● Method 2: Choose the first eight cereals from each shelf.

● Method 3: Number the cereals from 1 to 77. Use two spinners with equal sections numbered 0–9 to produce 25 different two-digit numbers. Choose the cereals corresponding to these numbers.

a. Which method is an example of convenience sampling?

b. Which method is an example of random sampling?

c. Which method is an example of systematic sampling?

d. Which method would you recommend? Explain.

3. The health class randomly selects 50 of the 600 students in their school. They ask these students the following questions:

- Question 1: On how many school days last week did you eat cereal for breakfast?

- Question 2: Do you prefer sweetened or unsweetened cereal?

   a. Of the students in the sample, 14 give answers of 4 or 5 to the first question. How many students in the entire school would you predict ate cereal on 4 or 5 days last week?

   b. Of the students in the sample, 32 say they prefer sweetened cereal. How many students in the school would you expect to prefer sweetened cereal?

Explain Your Reasoning

When you compare data sets, read graphs, choose samples, and use samples to make predictions, you should be able to justify your procedures and conclusions.

4. In what types of situations are box plots useful tools?

5. In what types of situations are scatter plots useful tools?

6. When does it make sense to use data from a sample to study a population?

7. Describe three kinds of sampling methods and their strengths and weaknesses.

8. How could you choose a random sample?

Statistical techniques for collecting and displaying data and drawing conclusions are used in nearly every branch of science, business, and government work. You will extend and use your statistical understanding and skills in your classes, in your future jobs, and in your everyday life.

B

box-and-whisker plot (or box plot) A display that shows the distribution of values in a data set separated into four equal-size groups. A box plot is constructed from the five-number summary of the data. The box plot below shows the distribution of quality ratings for natural brands of peanut butter.

gráfica de caja y brazos (o diagrama de caja) Una representación que muestra la distribución de valores de un conjunto de datos separada en cuatro grupos de igual tamaño. Una gráfica de caja y brazos se construye con el resumen de cinco números del conjunto de datos. La siguiente gráfica de caja y brazos representa la distribución de las calificaciones según la calidad de distintas marcas de mantequillas de maní.

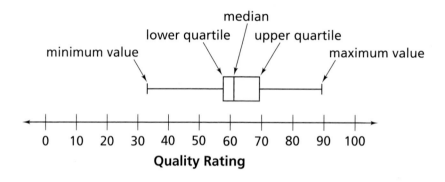

C

convenience sampling Choosing a sample because it is convenient. If you survey everyone on your soccer team who attends tonight's practice, you are surveying a convenience sample.

muestra de conveniencia Una muestra seleccionada porque es conveniente. Si entrevistaras a todos los integrantes de tu equipo de fútbol que asistan a la práctica esta noche, estarás encuestando una muestra de conveniencia.

D

distribution The arrangement of values in a data set.

distribución La disposición de valores en un conjunto de datos.

F

five-number summary The minimum value, lower quartile, median, upper quartile, and maximum value for a data set. These five values give a summary of the shape of the distribution and are used to make box plots. The five-number summary for the quality ratings for regular brands of peanut butter is as follows:

minimum value = 11
lower quartile = 31
median = 40
upper quartile = 54
maximum value = 83

resumen de cinco números El valor mínimo, el cuartil inferior, la mediana, el cuartil superior y el valor máximo de un conjunto de datos. Estos cinco valores dan un resumen de la forma de una distribución y se usan para hacer diagramas de caja. El resumen de cinco números para la calificación de calidad de las marcas de mantequilla de maní común es el siguiente:

valor mínimo = 11
cuartil inferior = 31
mediana = 40
cuartil superior = 54
valor máximo = 83

histogram A display that shows the distribution of numeric data. The range of data values, divided into intervals, is displayed on the horizontal axis. The vertical axis shows frequency in numbers or in percents. The height of the bar over each interval indicates the count or percent of data values in that interval. The histogram below shows quality ratings for regular brands of peanut butter. The height of the bar over the interval from 20 to 30 is 4. This indicates that four brands of peanut butter have quality ratings between 20 and 30.

histograma Una representación que muestra la distribución de datos numéricos. El rango de valores de los datos, dividido en intervalos, se representa en el eje horizontal. El eje vertical muestra la frecuencia en número o en porcentajes. La altura de la barra sobre cada intervalo indica el número, o porcentaje, de valores de datos en ese intervalo. El siguiente histograma representa la calificación por calidad de las marcas de mantequilla de maní común. La altura de la barra sobre el intervalo de 20 a 30 es 4. Esto indica que cuatro marcas de mantequilla de maní tienen una calificación entre 20 y 30.

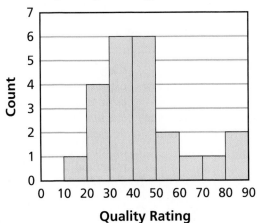

Quality of Regular Brands

lower quartile The median of the data values to the left of the median (assuming the values are listed from least to greatest). For example, consider an odd number of data values:

1, 2, 5, 6, 7, 8, 8, 10, 12, 15, 20

There are 11 data values. The median of the data set is 8. (Six values are at or above 8 and six are at or below 8.) The median of the values to the left of the median (1, 2, 5, 6, 7) is 5. So, the lower quartile is 5.

Consider an even number of data values:
2, 3, 4, 5, 6, 6, 8, 8

There are eight data values. The median of the data set is 5.5, the average of 5 and 6. The data values to the left of the median are 2, 3, 4, and 5. The median of these values is 3.5. So, the lower quartile is 3.5.

cuartil inferior La mediana del valor de los datos a la izquierda de la mediana (asumiendo que los valores indicados van de menor a mayor). Por ejemplo, consideremos un número impar de valores de datos:

1, 2, 5, 6, 7, 8, 8, 10, 12, 15, 20

Hay 11 valores de datos. La mediana del conjunto de datos es 8. (Seis valores están en o sobre 8 y seis están en o bajo 8.) La mediana de los valores a la izquierda de la mediana es (1, 2, 5, 6, 7) es 5. De modo que el cuartil inferior es 5.

Consideremos un número par de valores de datos:
2, 3, 4, 5, 6, 6, 8, 8

Hay ocho valores de datos. La mediana del conjunto de datos es 5.5, el promedio de 5 y 6. Los valores de los datos a la izquierda de la mediana son 2, 3, 4 y 5. La mediana de estos valores es 3.5. De modo que el cuartil inferior es 3.5.

population The entire collection of people or objects you are studying.

población Un conjunto entero de personas u objetos en estudio.

random sampling Choosing a sample in a way that gives every sample from a population an equally likely chance of being selected.

muestra aleatoria Elegir una muestra de manera que se dé a cada miembro de una población la misma posibilidad de ser elegido.

sample A group of people or objects selected from a population.

muestra Un grupo de personas u objetos seleccionados de una población.

sampling distribution The distribution of the means (or medians) of a set of same-size samples selected randomly from the same population.

distribución de muestra Distribución de las medias (o medianas) de un conjunto de muestras del mismo tomaño, seleccionadas al azar de la misma población.

scatter plot A graph used to explore the relationship between two variables. The graph below is a scatter plot of (*quality rating, price per serving*) for several peanut butters. Each point represents the quality rating and price per serving for one peanut butter.

diagrama de dispersión Una gráfica usada para explorar la relación entre dos variables. El siguiente es un diagrama de dispersión (*clasificación de calidad, precio por porción*) para varias mantequillas de cacahuate. Cada punto representa la clasificación de calidad y el precio por porción de una mantequilla de cacahuate.

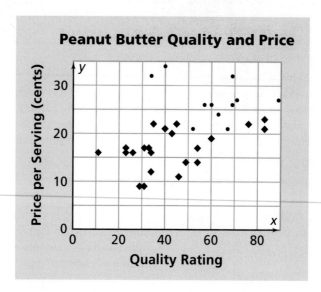

stem-and-leaf plot (or stem plot) A display that shows the distribution of values in a data set. Unlike a box plot or a histogram, a stem plot allows you to see the individual values in the data set. The stem plot below shows the distribution of quality ratings for regular brands of peanut butter. In this plot, the stems are a vertical list of the tens digits of the ratings. Attached to each stem are the corresponding leaves, in this case the ones digits. The leaves 3, 3, 6, and 9 next to the stem 2 indicate that the data set includes the values 23, 23, 26, and 29.

diagrama de tallo y hojas Una representación que muestra la distribución de valores en un conjunto de datos. A diferencia de una gráfica de caja y brazos o un histograma, un diagrama de tallo y hojas permite ver los valores individuales de un conjunto de datos. El diagrama de tallo y hojas siguiente muestra la distribución de la calificación por calidad de las marcas de mantequilla de maní común. En este diagrama, los tallos son una lista vertical de los dígitos de las decenas de las calificaciones. Unidas a cada tallo están las hojas correspondientes, en este caso, los dígitos de las unidades. Las hojas 3, 3, 6 y 9 al lado del tallo 2, indican que el conjunto de datos incluye los valores 23, 23, 26, and 29.

**Quality Ratings
of Regular
Peanut Butters**

Stem	Leaves
0	
1	1
2	3 3 6 9
3	1 1 3 4 4 5
4	0 0 3 5 6 9
5	4 4
6	0
7	6
8	3 3
9	

Key: 2 | 6 means 26

systematic sampling Choosing a sample in a methodical way. If you survey every tenth person on an alphabetical list of names, you are surveying a systematic sample.

muestra sistemática Una muestra seleccionada de una manera metódica. Si entrevistaras a cada décima persona en una lista de nombres en orden alfabético, estarías encuestando una muestra sistemática.

upper quartile The median of the data values to the right of the median (assuming the values are listed from least to greatest). For example, consider an odd number of data values:

1, 2, 5, 6, 7, 8, 8, 10, 12, 15, 20

There are 11 data values. The median of the data set is 8. The median of the values to the right of the median (8, 10, 12, 15, and 20) is 12. So, the upper quartile is 12.

Consider an even number of data values:
2, 3, 4, 5, 6, 6, 8, 8

There are eight data values. The median of the data set is 5.5, the average of 5 and 6. The data values to the right of the median are 6, 6, 8, 8. The median of these values is 7. So, the upper quartile is 7.

cuartil superior La mediana de los valores de los datos a la derecha de la mediana (asumiendo que los valores están indicados de menor a mayor). Por ejemplo, consideremos un número impar de valores de datos:

1, 2, 5, 6, 7, 8, 8, 10, 12, 15, 20

Hay 11 valores de datos. La mediana del conjunto de datos es 8. La mediana de los valores a la derecha de la mediana (8, 10, 12, 15, y 20) es 12. De modo que el cuartil superior es 12.

Consideremos un número par de valores de datos:
2, 3, 4, 5, 6, 6, 8, 8

Hay ocho valores de datos. La mediana del conjunto de datos es 5.5, el promedio de 5 y 6. Los valores de los datos a la derecha de la mediana son 6, 6, 8, 8. La mediana de estos valores es 7. De modo que el cuartil superior es 7.

voluntary-response sample A sample that selects itself. If you put an ad in the school paper asking for volunteers to take a survey, the students who respond will be a voluntary-response sample.

muestra de respuesta voluntaria Una muestra que se selecciona a sí misma. Si pones un anuncio en el periódico escolar pidiendo voluntarios para participar en una encuesta, los estudiantes que respondan serán una muestra de respuestas voluntarias.

Academic Vocabulary

The following terms are important to your understanding of the mathematics in this unit. Knowing and using these words will help you in thinking, reasoning, representing, communicating your ideas, and making connections across ideas. When these words make sense to you, the investigations and problems will make more sense as well.

D

describe To explain or tell in detail. A written description can contain facts and other information needed to communicate your answer. A diagram or a graph may also be included.
related terms: express, explain, illustrate

Sample: The band members want to conduct a survey. Describe a plan that uses systematic sampling.

> The band members can randomly select a starting time and then survey every sixth student who enters the school. This gives every student an equal chance of being selected.

describir Explicar o decir con detalle. Una descripción escrita puede contener hechos y otra información necesaria para comunicar tu respuesta. También se puede incluir un diagrama o una gráfica.
términos relacionados: expresar, explicar, ilustrar

Ejemplo: Los integrantes de una banda desean realizar una encuesta. Describe un plan que use la muestra sistemática.

> Los integrantes de la banda pueden seleccionar al azar un tiempo de inicio y luego aplicar la encuesta a cada sexto estudiante que entre a la escuela. Esto da a todos los estudiantes una oportunidad igual de ser seleccionado.

E

estimate To find an approximate answer.
related terms: approximate, guess

Sample: A cup manufacturer knows that approximately 4 out of every 2,000 cups are defective. Estimate how many of 10,000 cups bought by a restaurant will be defective.

> I can write 4 out of 2,000 as a percent.
> $\frac{4}{2,000} = 0.002 = 0.2\%$
> Then I can multiply 10,000 by 0.2% to estimate the number of defective cups bought by the restaurant chain.
> $0.002 \times 10,000 = 20$
> About 20 of the cups are defective.
> I can also use a proportion.
> $\frac{4}{2,000} = \frac{x}{10,000}$
> $2,000x = 40,000$
> $x = 20$

estimar Hallar una respuesta aproximada.
términos relacionados: aproximar, conjeturar

Ejemplo: Un fabricante de tazas sabe que aproximadamente 4 de cada 2,000 tazas están defectuosas. Estima cuántas de las 10,000 tazas compradas por un restaurante estarán defectuosas.

> Puedo escribir 4 de 2,000 como un porcentaje. $\frac{4}{2,000} = 0.002 = 0.2\%$
> Luego puedo multiplicar 10,000 por 0.2% para estimar el número de tazas defectuosas compradas por el restaurante.
> $0.002 \times 10,000 = 20$
> Alrededor de 20 de las tazas están defectuosas.
> También puedo usar una proporción.
> $\frac{4}{2,000} = \frac{x}{10,000}$
> $2,000x = 40,000$
> $x = 20$

expect To use theoretical or experimental data to anticipate a certain outcome.

related terms: anticipate, predict

Sample: A cook makes trail mix in 2-pound batches. She puts a bag of almonds into each batch. There are about 120 almonds in each bag. Explain how many almonds you would expect to find in one-half pound of trail mix.

> If I divide 2 pounds of trail mix into half-pound parts, I will have 4 parts. Since the cook puts 120 almonds into each batch, divide 120 by 4 to determine the expected number of almonds in one-half pound. I can expect to find 30 almonds in one-half pound of trail mix because 120 ÷ 4 = 30.

esperar Usar datos teóricos o experimentales para anticipar un determinado resultado.

términos relacionados: anticipar, predecir

Ejemplo: Una cocinera hace un cóctel de frutos secos en lotes de 2 libras. Pone una bolsa de almendras en cada lote. Hay alrededor de 120 almendras en cada bolsa. Explica cuántas almendras esperarías hallar en media libra de cóctel de frutos secos.

> Si divido 2 libras de cóctel de frutos secos en partes de media libra, tendré 4 partes. Puesto que la cocinera pone 120 almendras en cada lote, divido 120 entre 4 para determinar el número esperado de almendras en media libra. Puedo esperar hallar 30 almendras en media libra de cóctel de frutos secos porque 120 ÷ 4 = 30

---

explain To give facts and details that make an idea easier to understand. Explaining can involve a written summary supported by a diagram, chart, table, or a combination of these.

related terms: analyze, clarify, describe, justify, tell

Sample: Explain why the line graph is misleading.

Number of 8th Grade Students

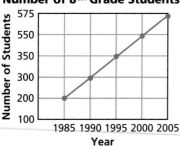

> The vertical axis of the graph does not start with zero and does not increase by the same amount for each interval. This causes the data to appear to increase at a constant rate, but it is increasing at different rates. Therefore, the graph is misleading.

explicar Dar hechos y detalles que hacen que una idea sea más fácil de comprender. Explicar puede implicar un resumen escrito apoyado por un diagrama, una gráfica, una tabla o una combinación de éstos.

términos relacionados: analizar, aclarar, describir, justificar, decir

Ejemplo: Explica por qué la gráfica lineal es engañosa.

Número de estudiantes del grado 8

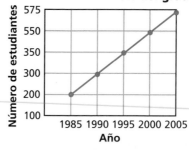

> El eje vertical de la gráfica no empieza con cero y no se incrementa por la misma cantidad para cada intervalo. Esto causa que los datos parezcan aumentar con una relación constante, pero está aumentando con relaciones diferentes. Por consiguiente, la gráfica es engañosa.

Index

Index   **93**

Acknowledgments

Team Credits

The people who made up the **Connected Mathematics 2** team—representing editorial, editorial services, design services, and production services—are listed below. Bold type denotes core team members.

Leora Adler, Judith Buice, Kerry Cashman, Patrick Culleton, Sheila DeFazio, Richard Heater, **Barbara Hollingdale, Jayne Holman,** Karen Holtzman, **Etta Jacobs,** Christine Lee, Carolyn Lock, Catherine Maglio, **Dotti Marshall,** Rich McMahon, Eve Melnechuk, Kristin Mingrone, Terri Mitchell, **Marsha Novak,** Irene Rubin, Donna Russo, Robin Samper, Siri Schwartzman, **Nancy Smith,** Emily Soltanoff, **Mark Tricca,** Paula Vergith, Roberta Warshaw, Helen Young

Additional Credits

Diana Bonfilio, Mairead Reddin, Michael Torocsik, nSight, Inc.

Photographs

Every effort has been made to secure permission and provide appropriate credit for photographic material. The publisher deeply regrets any omission and pledges to correct errors called to its attention in subsequent editions.

Unless otherwise acknowledged, all photographs are the property of Pearson Education, Inc.

Photo locators denoted as follows: Top (T), Center (C), Bottom (B), Left (L), Right (R), Background (Bkgd)

2 (T) Kristy-Anne Glubish/Design Pics Inc./ Alamy, (B) david tipling/Alamy; **3** Fritz Polking/ The Image Works, Inc.; **5** ACE STOCK LIMITED/Alamy Images; **7** Michael Newman/ PhotoEdit, Inc.; **16** Nicole Katano/AGE Fotostock; **21** SW Productions/PhotoDisc/Getty Images; **24** (C) Dean Fox/SuperStock, (C) Visions of America/SuperStock; **26** Spencer Grant/PhotoEdit, Inc.; **27** ©Rob Melnychuk/ Getty Images; **35** Max Oppenheim/Stone/Getty Images; **37** Kristy-Anne Glubish/Design Pics Inc./ Alamy; **39** image100/SuperStock; **43** Bob Johns/ Alamy Images; **47** Alberto Paredes/Alamy Images; **48** Hemera Technologies/Alamy; **50** SuperStock/ AGE Fotostock; **51** (B) Gary Conner/Index Stock Imagery/PhotoLibrary Group, Inc.; **54** Hemera Technologies/Alamy; **56** Peter Casolino/ Alamy Images; **58** David Mendelsohn/Masterfile Corporation; **65** Brakefield Photo/ PictureQuest/ Jupiter Images; **71** Hemera Technologies/Alamy; **74** agorulko/ Shutterstock; **79** altrendo nature/ Getty Images; **81** david tipling/Alamy

Technical Illustration

WestWords, Inc.

Cover Design

tom white.images

Data Sources

Grateful acknowledgement is made to the following for copyrighted material:

Consumers Union

"The Nuttiest Peanut Butter" Copyright 1990 by Consumers Union of U.S., Inc., Yonkers, NY 10703-1057, a nonprofit organization. Reprinted with permission from the September 1990 issue of CONSUMER REPORTS® for educational purposes only. (p 6)

The Food Commission

Data from *"Parents Beware: Juice in Juice Drinks costs up to £34 per litre"* from WWW.FOODCOMM.ORG.UK/LOWJUICE_ 04.HTM#PURE (p 21)

NBA Entertainment

"Houston Rockets 2004 Roster" and *"Chicago Bulls 2004 Roster"* from WWW.NBA.COM. Reprinted with the permission of NBA Entertainment. (p 23)

Acknowledgments

Data Sources (continued)

GfK Mediamark Research & Intelligence, LLC

From *"Nuts About Peanut Butter ("The average kid eats 1,500 peanut butter sandwiches...")"* from NEWSWEEK, SEPTEMBER 14, 1998. Used by permission of GfK Mediamark Research & Intelligence, LLC. (p 27)

The Institute of General Semantics

From *"Adolescents and their music ("Between Grades 7 and 12...")"* by Sheila Davis from ET CETERA, SUMMER 1985. Reprinted with permission of the Institute of General Semantics, Forest Hills, N.Y. (p 27)

Consumers Union

"Memo to Members by Rhoda H. Karpatkin" Copyright 1998 by Consumers Union of U.S., Inc., Yonkers, NY 10703-1057, a nonprofit organization. Reprinted with permission from the February 1998 issue of CONSUMER REPORTS® for educational purposes only. (p 27)

George C. Knight

From *"Site 1 and Site 2 Arrowhead Sizes"* by George C. Knight and James D. Keyser from PLAINS ANTHROPOLOGIST VOLUME 28, NUMBER 101, 1983. Reprinted by permission of the author. (p 48)

From *"A Mathematical Technique for Dating Projectile Points Common to the Northwestern Plains (Big Goose Creek Arrowheads)"* by George C. Knight and James D. Keyser from PLAINS ANTHROPOLOGIST VOLUME 28, NUMBER 101, 1983. Reprinted by permission of the author. (p 49)

From *"A Mathematical Technique for Dating Projectile Points Common to the Northwestern Plains (Wortham Shelter Arrowheads)"* by George C. Knight and James D. Keyser from PLAINS ANTHROPOLOGIST VOLUME 28, NUMBER 101, 1983. Reprinted by permission of the author. (p 49)

From *"A Mathematical Technique for Dating Projectile Points Common to the Northwestern Plains (Kobold/Buffalo Creek Arrowheads)"* by George C. Knight and James D. Keyser from PLAINS ANTHROPOLOGIST VOLUME 28, NUMBER 101, 1983. Reprinted by permission of the author. (pp 49 and 71)

American Forest and Paper Association

Data from the *"Recovery of ONP/Mechanical Papers"* from www.paperrecycles.org. Used by permission. (p 57)

Plymouth Press, Ltd.

"Airplane Comparisons by Engine, Body Length and Wingspan" by William and Frank Berk from GUIDE TO AIRPORT AIRPLANES (p 64)